Crime, Corruption & Capacity in Papua New Guinea

Crime, Corruption & Capacity in Papua New Guinea

Maxine Pitts

Asia Pacific Press
at The Australian National University

Published by
Asia Pacific Press
Asia Pacific School of Economics and Management
The Australian National University
Canberra ACT 0200
Ph: 61-2-6125 4700 Fax: 61-2-6257 2886
Website: http://www.asiapacificpress.com

National Library of Australia Cataloguing in Publication entry

Pitts, Maxine, 1950-.
Crime, corruption and capacity.

Bibliography.
ISBN 0 7315 3681 9.

1. Criminal justice, Administration of - Papua New Guinea. 2. Crime prevention - Papua New Guinea. 3. Crime - Papua New Guinea. 4. Political corruption - Papua New Guinea. I. Title.

364.9953

Production: Asia Pacific Press
Cover Design: Annie di Nallo
Printed in Australia by Southwood Press

Contents

Tables

Symbols used in tables

..	not available
n.a.	not applicable
-	zero
.	insignificant

Abbreviations

A-GD	Department of Attorney-General
ANZ	Australia and New Zealand Banking Group Ltd
AusAID	Australian Agency for International Development
CODE	College of Distance Education
DAL	Department of Agriculture and Livestock
EHP	Eastern Highlands Province
EU	European Union
GDP	gross domestic product
HIV/AIDs	Human Immunodeficiency Virus/Acquired Immunodeficiency Syndrome
IMF	International Monetary Fund
JICA	Japan International Cooperation Agency
LISP	Legal Institutions Strengthening Project
LLG	local level government
MP	Member of Parliament
NCD	National Capital District
NEC	National Executive Council
NGO	non-government organisation
NSO	National Statistics Office
PIP	Public Investment Program
PMRG	Project Monitoring and Review Group
PMV	passenger motor vehicle
PNG	Papua New Guinea
PNGCS	Papua New Guinea Correctional Service
PNGDF	Papua New Guinea Defence Force
RDB	Rural Development Bank
RDP	Rural Development Program
RPNGC	Royal Papua New Guinea Constabulary
RPNGCDP	Royal Papua New Guinea Constabulary Development Project
SBDC	Small Business Development Corporation
TP	'Tokpisin', English Pidgin lauguage which is a major *lingua franca* in Papua New Guinea
UN	United Nations
US	United States
WHP	Western Highlands Province

Acknowledgments

I dedicate this book to the people of Papua New Guinea who have taught me and guided me in my assumptions and learning of whom they are and what they want as individuals and as a nation. There are many people I would like to thank. First, Dr Michael Goddard for his patience and perseverance in guiding me in an unobtrusive, measured way during the first, significant part of my journey by challenging me and toning down my sometimes long-winded phrases when the content was in the form a Master of Arts thesis.

Many others showed interest in what I was attempting, helped me to access information, gave their time for interviews and general opinions, facilitated contacts, listened to, queried and corrected my various assumptions and inspired me generally. These people include: the former Commissioner for the PNG Correctional Service Ken Serupi who gave me permission to access organisational information for research purposes, Michael Heaven, Bill Kidston, Will Glynn, Jim Benn, Roslyn Stewart and Teresa O'Donnell, John and Judy Tara, Dominique Tomar, Thaddy Ambing, Benedict Kasi, Godfrey Niggints, Kaisa Kamewawa, Michael Mosiri, Kelly Karella, Kiddy and Mary Keko, Molly Moihau, Regina Cooper, Geoffrey Padawa, Michael Joseph, Robert Sirai, Muli Kenakena, Archie Vanua, David Sipitai, Michael Turner, Janet Regione, Robin Chalker, Kevin Rauie, Ken Skews, Rosemary Robertson, Lady Carol Kidu, Larry George, Kevin Murphy, Kepas Paun, Kaoru Miyahara, Thomas Chien, Ian Mopafi who, as my friends and colleagues acted as sounding boards for my ideas, challenged my assumptions and arguments, and gave their opinions unreservedly. I am particularly indebted to the late Alfred Bala who gave his time often and freely to discuss and give advice on crime prevention issues and to his wife Leako. I am also indebted to Sinclair Dinnen and David Boorer who showed me how to start my journey and to the Brigadene Sisters of Maino Heduru from whom I gained many insights.

I am also grateful to others who took an interest in my research, were generous with their time and participated actively in facilitating contacts, enabling interviews and discussing issues. They include: Augustine and Mary Mac, all Chiefs, Councillors and church representatives at Woitape and especially Brother Andrew Anama and John Inne, the Woitape health officer and her family, Linda Rau and her family, Paul and Taita for their hospitality, the Chief of all Chiefs Naimo Ikupu and other chiefs of Kivori poe, United Church delegates and youth group members from the Delena Circuit, Stoney Daure Maraga, Gabutu Gaudi, Temu Elly, Rarua Gamu, other Motu-Koita village Court Magistrates and Councillors, Mike Manning, Lohia Raka, Peter Moimo and his family, Wayne Golding, Michael O'Connell, Graham McKenzie, Bob Mellor, Paul Loki, Phillip Son, Erwin Wilhelm, Bill Kavulio, Lawrence Newell, Salvation Army Juvenile Centre officers, Hohola Youth Centre officers, John Waliapan, Patrick Haiya, Lima Ohohpare, Narai Billy and his team and various incarcerated persons whom I am unable to name. There are others who have contributed indirectly to the formation of arguments and insights, especially the staff and prisoners of the PNG Correctional Service, police personnel, community correctional officers of the Department of the Attorney-General, Magistrates and Judges, Provincial Administrators, other Local Level Government Councillors, church, women's and youth group representatives to whom I am also grateful.

I wish also to thank my father Max who stood by me, my late mother Maree who believed in me, my daughters, Celeste and Ruth and my granddaughter Clare for their love, patience and support, my sons, Adam, Sam and Shane, Michele, Sam's wife, Erin, Shane's wife, Julius and August, Sam and Michele's sons, Ruby and Darla, Shane and Erin's daughters and Erin's mum Jill for their geographically distant interest in this project which seemed never ending.

To Colin Hunt, my partner in life, who tolerated my moods,

nurtured and encouraged me, cooked wonderful meals, listened to me, challenged flawed arguments, helped me to edit my final words and inspired me to stay healthy and relatively sane throughout the highs and lows of the writing experience, and to my dog Kujo who lay patiently at my feet throughout the journey, thank you. And to the publishing team of Asia Pacific Press, headed by Maree Tait, thank you for the opportunity to publish this work. The editing and pagesetting skills of Wendy Lown are also acknowledged.

Maxine Patricia Pitts
Port Moresby
Papua New Guinea
November 2001

Introduction

Years of junketing, greed, sloth, sheer incompetence and outright corruption which pilfers workers' superannuation funds and implicates a former prime minister and a former finance minister for alleged public graft and deception is sending Papua New Guinea into an economic tailspin. The Prime Ministerial efforts of the Morauta Government to pull Papua New Guinea back from the brink of bankruptcy, include taking several provincial governments to task, withdrawing administrative powers and calling upon others to show cause as to why their powers should not be withdrawn (Ricketts 2000). Commissions of inquiry into massive fraud and structural reform of the public sector have also been initiated, showing the strength and tenacity of the Prime Minister for retribution in Papua New Guinea can be swift and fatal, and showing that the Office of the Prime Minister is one of insecure tenure within the maze of ethnic factionalism, rivalry and jealousies, that is politics and governance.

Despite the economic plight of their country, PNG politicians voted themselves and other constitutional office holders a pay rise in February 2001. While their rate of pay is below that of Australian politicians, the extra expenditure is something the country cannot afford. The pay rise gives an ordinary MP a weekly salary of K1,600 (A$752) and the Prime Minister K3,173 (A$1,491) over and above housing, motor vehicle, travel and other allowances. This is in stark contrast with the PNG Minimum Wages Board decision in the same year to increase the weekly basic wage to K72.20 (A$34). The vast gap between the official bottom wage line and politicians' pay rises does not sit well with many PNG citizens (Callaghan 2001). Students at the University of Papua New Guinea called on the Salaries and Remuneration Commission to rescind its decision to approve increases to parliamentarians and other constitutional office holders because 'the salaries' are 'a big fat slap in the face' for the majority suffering in silence. Former Prime Minister, Sir Rabbie Namaliu, said payments and payouts to some senior officials—who are 'political appointees (and) not worth a fraction of what they are paid'—are excessive and he wants parliament to backdate a law to ban such payments and payouts; some, he says earn between K400,000 and K1 million a year.

Communities absorb such justifications and arguments, rational and irrational. Marginalised citizens feel victimised, and in an effort to gain and maintain personal power and a greater share of resources, mimic the behaviour of their leaders—behaviour that often manifests in crime, corrupt practice and low productivity. The control of crime is very difficult because the level of control by both the state and communities is a manifestation of shared values, opinions and pressures, and is often politically influenced, biased, prompted by fear of negative sanctions, and influenced by the need for state resources.

State capacity dictates community capacity and community capacity is governed by leadership integrity, resource equity and availability. This means that if the capacity of the state is weak, the capacity of communities is weak, as communities are limited by the same ingrained problems that inhibit state initiatives to control crime. Ingrained problems may relate to obligations of political and clan alliances, and imbalanced resources caused by corrupt, poor, or non-existent distribution of goods and services to citizens. Papua New Guinea is a constitutional democracy. It has a free press and in theory, free speech. Citizens are informed through the print and electronic media and are encouraged by the media to give their opinions. Letters to the editors of local newspapers are often passionate about issues relating to criminality and the corrupt practice of persons in positions of trust. Speaking out in this way is relatively safe for the ordinary citizen and stimulating for readers. However, there is a general fear of being too direct over a prolonged period about the aberrant behaviour of some leaders and their amassed wealth that manifests itself in expensive vehicles, Australian real estate and Australian boarding school education for their children.

Papua New Guinea citizens are distressed that transparent, trustworthy and firm leadership which keeps citizens informed, reaches consensus of vision with citizens, works with citizens to alleviate social and economic constraints, supports citizens in practical terms to achieve goals, practises fiscal and other discipline, and supports prosecution of fraudulent leaders, rarely occurs. Both government and community-based development initiatives remain donor dependent; allegations of corruption and mismanagement against politicians and administrators are frequent; and communities often express detachment from state process and disinterest in state-driven crime control strategies. There is also a tendency to externalise problems and blame foreigners for the country's troubles. The most popular scapegoats are the multilateral agencies like the World Bank and the International Monetary Fund whose agenda is to instil fiscal discipline into the PNG economy—without which it will not survive. The June 2001 protests of rioting university students against the government's privatisation agenda and media reports of disgruntled citizens, indicate that many Papua New Guineans do not fully realise the devastating social and economic implications should privatisation of certain government and semi-government institutions not occur. Quite simply, bailouts are over, and Papua New Guinea will face bankruptcy unless the government divests itself of its inefficient, loss-making functions.

Fundamentalist and egocentric politicians, who sway citizens into a false sense of security—that they can 'go back to the land' and that they 'don't need foreigners'—are doing them a grave disservice. If acted upon, it will ultimately backfire in greater social and economic upheaval caused by deprivation of basic human rights like water, food, shelter, health, education and opportunity. Papua New Guinea is irretrievably part of the global political, economic and social community. Until its leaders have the courage to set honourable, personal standards of complying with agreements with international agencies who have bailed them out, and make the hard economic and administrative decisions required to do so, foreign investors, aid and lending agencies will continue to withdraw. The PNG economy, already overburdened by an exploding population and an HIV epidemic will stagnate because sick, uneducated, uninformed citizens with low life expectancies are not productive.

Some PNG citizens say independence came too soon: 'we were not ready'; 'we didn't have to fight for it'; 'we still rely on handouts'. An increasing number say they would have preferred to remain under the Australian regime as a self-governing territory until a knowledge base had been built up and greater familiarisation with Western systems of government had occurred. They believe PNG citizens could have benefited more from Australian education systems, health care and general guidance and support. Instead, Australian colonial legacies to Papua New Guinea at Independence on 16 September 1975 were weak administrative systems, foreign laws—often at odds with customary laws—and an élite PNG minority representing only one per cent of citizens. This tiny élite was tasked with creating nationhood from over seven hundred culturally and politically diverse language groups in a post-independent environment of rapid urban migration, population explosions, a stagnant economy, growing unemployment and increasingly frequent and vicious crime.

Reported crime rose steadily from the early 1970s when the PNG economy began to stagnate, fewer jobs became available and opportunities to go to school, or continue in school after grade six, diminished. Efforts to contain crime have been many and varied, ranging from raiding and burning by police to the pursuit of bridging mechanisms between the state and communities. These mechanisms include village courts, community policing, and law and order committees. Most mechanisms continue to flounder. The main reason for this is that initiatives are often devoid of leader support at national and local levels; that is, devoid of leaders whose integrity manifests in adequate and consistent resource input to provide for and inform citizens, allay fears, ignorance and jealousy, and prosecute and punish defrauders of the public purse. While some efforts are being made to instil greater accountability and to back pay public servants, development initiatives and service delivery are often hampered severely by inefficient and corrupt administrative regimes.

The Electricity Commission is in enormous debt and the national capital is subject to rolling electricity cuts. The National Capital City Commission (the city council), Post Papua New Guinea Limited (the postal service) and Motor Vehicles Insurance Limited are all bankrupt. Not even the Privatisation Commission has escaped unscathed and may be put in receivership to enforce debt payments. The estimated cost of the privatisation program in 2001 was K178 million. By October 2001 none of the entities earmarked for sale under the program had been sold. In consequence, World Bank funds of US$20 million for the structural adjustment program, tied specifically to bringing Papua New Guinea Banking Corporation to the point of sale, had not been released.

Papua New Guinea has a Westminster legal system that the state administers. It seeks to control crime by apprehending offenders and prosecuting them in courts. Courts may order monetary penalties, good behaviour bonds, suspended prison sentences, probation and community service, or jail. Criminal justice agencies like the police, courts, probation and parole services and prisons are delegated to protect the community from offences against state law. Their core business is to apprehend, prosecute, punish and rehabilitate offenders to encourage them to participate in society in legitimate ways. Five government agencies constitute the state crime control structure. Their administration is centralised and their players are heterogeneous. These agencies are the Department of Justice (magistrates, district, and supreme courts, called the National Courts), the Royal Papua New Guinea Constabulary (RPNGC), Papua New Guinea Correctional Service (PNGCS), Department of the Attorney-General (A-GD) and Department of Home Affairs. Police arrest offenders and prosecute them in the magistrates court. National Court magistrates and judges make judgements in relation to sentencing, and the correctional service incarcerates offenders in response to court orders. Officers delegated by the A-GD have several roles: to prosecute offenders; provide legal aid to offenders facing imprisonment; advise the National Executive Council (NEC) and state agencies on legal matters; administer community courts; advise magistrates and judges on community based sentencing options; and supervise offenders on community based orders. Delegated officers of the Department of Home Affairs oversee the care and rehabilitation of juvenile offenders.

State criminal justice agencies are badly under-resourced however and stagger in their efforts to control crime. Poorly administered or inappropriate management systems weaken them further, and reduce their capacity to keep up with the criminal manifestations of an exploding, culturally diverse population much of which is illiterate or poorly educated and has minimal access to health care, schools and jobs. As far back as the 1970s and early 1980s, concerns were raised regarding the increase in crime and the inability of criminal justice agencies to control it. In response, the then Prime Minister, Sir Michael Somare, commissioned what became known as the Clifford Report to review crime control strategies and make recommendations. A major recommendation of the report was the utilisation of customary social and economic structures, and value systems in crime control. This recommendation was made for two reasons. First, the authors of the report believed that Papua New Guinea has a strong sense of community that could be powerful if harnessed. Second, they believed state crime control agencies were highly politicised, corrupt and in constant conflict with one another, manifesting in poor relations between the state and its citizens. Criminologist Sinclair Dinnen echoed these sentiments in 1992, and seven years later remarked how ineffectual, under-resourced and over-stretched state controls are in containing rising levels of violence. He agreed particularly with the Clifford Report recommendation that Papua New Guinea's strong sense of community needs to be harnessed, because modernised customary laws wield significant influence at village level, and many disputes are settled outside the state legal system through informal mechanisms like village moots (Dinnen 1992:10–6, 1994a:3, 1999:37).

Papua New Guinea citizens say that while they utilise customary mechanisms to control crime in their families and communities, they want more support and interest from their government. They say the best way to achieve this is for leaders to set examples as moral citizens and to actively support crime control initiatives by providing resources to maintain them.

Many citizens express anguish regarding the frustrations and disillusionment of their youth. They say the hopelessness many young people feel manifests in criminality. Morata, a settlement-cum-suburb of Port Moresby, lost its health clinic to vandalism. 'Monkies' (grade six dropouts) smashed windows and walls and threw out and broke the equipment. They did this in anger because they see PNG 'big men' and expatriates driving around in expensive cars, living in nice houses, buying good food and having well-paid jobs, while they live in poverty. They try to go to school but are often sent home because teachers are absent. With nothing to do and few controls, they get up to mischief, *lusim gutpela tinktink* (Tok Pisin [TP]: do not think about good things) and smash government property like the health clinic. In Morata, it is commonly believed that 'rascals' have *strongpela guns* (TP: sophisticated weapons) 'stolen from the Papua New Guinea Defence Force' and because of this, police are too afraid to go there. On 9 October 2000, *Post-Courier* headlined, 'Gory killings stun city'. The 'gory killings' were the beheading of several youths at Morata, believed to be 'payback'[1] for a grenade killing of four people.

Though constantly undermined by meagre resource and leadership support, PNG citizens make considerable effort to maintain order in their communities and organisations. While efforts vary, village court arbitration appears to be the most common and most popular way to resolve community-based disputes. This is because disputes are resolved in the public arena of the community according to shared values and opinions. Arbitration by an elder, group of elders, church leader or other prominent persons outside a court is also popular. However certain decisions by village courts or other community arbitrators are not state sanctioned. Various government and non-government agencies develop and implement systems of accountability to prevent fraud or form self-help groups that create economic opportunity or social advancement, in attempts to control crime. Unfortunately, many initiatives are short-lived. Some communities form vigilante groups or employ security companies to keep peace. This relieves under-resourced, state crime control agencies. Others use 'traditional' methods to control crime. Some 'traditional' controls, however, are crimes against the state. They may include tribal fighting and paybacks that manifest in burglaries, car thefts, muggings, killings or sorcery. When the state arbitrates such cases in court, it often hands down sentences which may combine state administered penalties like imprisonment, with traditional controls like compensation and other agreed dispute resolution strategies. Police, provincial or local level governments and village courts often work together to implement strategies with a view to avoiding further violence.

Papua New Guinea is a weak state. This means it is a state depleted by frequent political leadership changes and corruption, manifesting in an increasing inability to provide goods and services to its citizens and an increasing inability to control crime. Public frustration caused by these phenomena often manifests in criminality and reinforces the need for community dispute resolution that may not always be appropriate. Communities, sick of the empty promises of the state, provide for their *lains* (TP: descent groups) by whatever means they can. Some rural communities sanction highway robberies and some politicians are said to be involved in highway-looting networks, reaping illicit material benefits that they use to humour voters and buy votes at election time. Meanwhile the state, floundering in its capacity to control crime, often reacts brutally. When this happens, communities become closed, withdraw support from state law and order agencies and mirror state sanctioned violence. State agencies, overwhelmed by pillage and burn rampages of angry individuals, communities and gangs, and under pressure 'to do something', resort to short-term, brutal, bandaid strategies. These actions simply reinforce community violence, build barriers to cooperation and 'marginalise' aggressors.

Sam Inguba, a senior police officer with the PNG Constabulary, said 'people blame the police for the law and order problem while the police blame a lack of funding and adequate resources'. The core problem he says is the lack of infrastructure and unequal access to basic goods and services for citizens. He cites Bob Nenta, a former police commissioner, who believes the law and order problem is more a symptom of deeper, underlying social dysfunction than a reflection of police operational methods (Inguba 1999:48–9). Yet the police raid on the home of a Lae family, who hosted the funeral of a man allegedly killed by police, is an indication that not all 'police operational methods' are desirable or effective. The *Post-Courier* report stated, 'the family was terrified because they were treated like animals' and 'some of them [the police] were drunk' (4 January 2000:2).

Sexual and other aggressive attacks on women and children are frequent, vicious and violent in Papua New Guinea. Vulnerable women and children, exploited sexually, are often blamed for the 'loss of face' of men or groups and 'need to be taught a lesson'. Authors Banks (2000) and Borrey (2000) warn against analysis of sexual crimes from a Western perspective, as the English words 'rape', 'sexual assault' and 'incest' have no equivalent words in PNG languages. Some sexual attacks are not considered crimes and victim trauma is often downplayed to relieve the shame on the victim's family. Compensation, retribution against the victim for encouraging the attack, or revenge attacks on the perpetrator or his family, are often the only perceived acceptable and honourable outcomes. These expected 'customary' outcomes often confound state law that protects the rights of women and children. This is because Western-oriented state law courts focus on victim pain and suffering, alien to expectations of allaying the 'loss of face'. As a result, many cases of sexual attack are not reported to the police and do not reach national courts, the victim's relatives often preventing the victim from testifying against the perpetrator in a national court of law, to ensure the desired compensation is ordered. Many victims do not object, as the outcome for them may otherwise be a beating, murder, or banishment from the family. The most popular way to deal with such cases is through village courts. In 1999, I was told that the rape of an adolescent village girl had been 'resolved' through the village court when the family of the victim was 'compensated'. The victim's family 'didn't want the matter to go any further' rendering both state and victim powerless to punish the perpetrator, recompense the victim for pain and suffering or uphold the rights of women. Some PNG writers say this is common, citing such cases as good examples of how state law is often at odds with customary laws (Hukula 1999:6, Sikani 1996:41).

The cost of crime to the state has been estimated at more than 4.6 per cent of gross domestic product (GDP) in direct costs. Total direct costs of larceny have been estimated at K61 million for the private sector and K29 million for the public sector. There are also substantial external costs as fear and anxiety mount and community mobility is confined to avoid attacks (Levantis and Chand 1997:4, World Bank 1999:111). Newspaper reports indicate that crime in Papua New Guinea is becoming more frequent and more violent—the police believe it is becoming 'more random and more vicious'. Certainly, the November 2001 ambush and pack rape of a 12-year old girl and the ambush and rape of four Air Nuigini female workers is indicative of a powerless society whose most vindictive members perpetrate insidious crimes on the most vulnerable (Yadi 2001, Dau 2001). In 1997 it was estimated that crime had risen '20-fold' over the past 20 years (Levantis 1997) and serious crime statistics in the second half of the 1990s indicated that such crimes were 65 per cent higher than 10 years before, averaging 11,500 a year. Criminal manifestations of a frustrated and rapidly growing youth population with minimal access to goods and services through legitimate means, puts pressure on resource deficient, highly politicised, poorly managed and inefficient law and order agencies, whose violent reactions erode public trust and propel youth into criminality. The situation has worsened since Dinnen (1992) made these observations. Reports of police bashings are common, national courts lumber under increasing demands, and meagre resources minimise community based sentencing options.

Factionalism, formed along ethnic and training group sub-cultural lines, is ingrained in law and order agencies. It impacts on senior officer appointments, distorts promotions board and discipline committee decisions, and discriminates severely against women. The *Post-Courier* headlined: 'Promotions ignite police tension', reporting that police were disgruntled over recent promotions claiming they were unfair and 'some of the people promoted did not deserve to be promoted' (6 January 2000:1). The same newspaper reported the next day that correctional officers were also disgruntled because officers with bad disciplinary and performance records, or those too old had been promoted. The report stated that nepotism was rife, and the PNGCS Commissioner was aware of the way the promotions had been made but had opted 'to do nothing' (*Post-Courier* 7–9 January 2000:2).

Half the prisoners in major PNG jails in 1999 were on remand awaiting court hearings. In September 2001, the number on remand had risen to 75 per cent (*Post-Courier* 26 September 2001) with escapes frequent and food for prisoners scarce. In March 2001, a prisoner who was part of a prison outreach program in Port Moresby, told school children that prisoners get so hungry they sometimes eat toothpaste; that green vegetables are rare; and that it is common for up to six prisoners to share one small tin of corn beef. Even though some commanding officers make committed attempts to provide nutritional diets, adequate living conditions and rehabilitation programs for inmates—in July 2001 there was talk of growing rice nationwide to feed prisoners and reduce ration costs—most jails are run down and prisoner facilities are appalling. While a goal of the Australian Agency for International Development (AusAID) funded project, working with the PNGCS, is to repair buildings and install a maintenance regime, consistent resource provision, and political and administrative skill and will, is needed to sustain it. On 17 November 1999, it was reported that the remand cell of Buimo jail in Lae was 'crammed', the next day, that 20 inmates had escaped and four days later, that an apprehended prisoner had '…died from injuries [he] sustained at the time of his recapture' (*The National* 17 November 1999:1, 18 November 1999:1, 22 November 1999:2). In February 2001, it was reported that the new PNGCS Commissioner, Richard Sikani, was 'angry' because 72 prisoners had escaped from the National Capital District (NCD) prison of Bomana over the last year and K14,000 'left in the hands of prison officers' had vanished. Of only 20 prisoners recaptured, two had died 'during recapture'. The Commissioner vowed to 'clean up' the organisation and two weeks later the same newspaper reported two foiled attempts by PNGCS staff to make illicit deposits of PNGCS cheques totalling K189,000 (*Post-Courier* 16–8 February 2001, 26–8 February, 6 March). Meanwhile, prisons continue to have difficulty getting remand prisoners to court due to 'fuel and funding problems'. One magistrate threatened to release such prisoners if they were not brought to court on time.

A dilemma of controlling crime in Papua New Guinea is that what may be a crime according to state law, may not be a crime according to local law, and what may be considered a minor crime by the state, is a serious crime under local law. For example, adultery is a criminal offence in Papua New Guinea, punishable by up to 12 months' imprisonment. In many PNG rural communities it is considered to be more serious than murder. On the other hand, sodomy, bestiality and bigamy are not regarded as serious offences (Clifford, Morauta and Stuart 1984a). Village courts, whose officials are untrained and often unpaid, arbitrate a wide range of matters (some of which are outside their jurisdiction). They order little or no community work, recommend prison sentences to higher courts for adultery and non-payment of fines, and fail to pursue the prosecution of perpetrators of serious crime. Instead, they bend to community demands for compensation and discriminate severely against women and children. The chairman of NCD village courts in 1998, said that while communities use village courts extensively, opposing parties do not agree to all court decisions, and some village court magistrates are considered 'easily influenced'. While aggrieved parties have recourse through national courts of law, retribution by such parties can occur in other ways. These may include sorcery, payback killings[1], muggings, rapes or property damage—some in the guise of tribal fighting. Such acts disrupt social order and create fear in communities. Some citizens participate in or condone such retribution while believing that community order and social advancement will occur through economic development. The dysfunctional link between the two results in community development project failure. Poor systems of management and accountability, and little or no government resource support may result in sabotage as a result of ignorance, infighting and jealousy.

Citizens who feel neglected perpetuate community controls that are not state sanctioned and do not offer long-term solutions. For example tribal fighting, which was outlawed in the late 1970s, remains an accepted first stage coercive community method of resolving conflict in some Highlands communities. Mutually agreed compensation by participating parties is the second stage of resolving conflict, and in traditional scenarios, such compensation assisted with the redistribution of goods. Prolonged tribal fighting using firearms however, has had disastrous social and economic effects on communities, closing off whole regions to sustainable economic advancement. Spasmodic fighting continues, and the social and economic capacity of the Southern Highlands, Enga and other highlands provinces remains weak. Populations, whose villages have been burned and whose gardens and livestock destroyed are confined, uneducated, sick and fearful. A man from the Nipa District in the Southern Highlands, said that fighting had divided families and dispersed communities, but the core reasons for disputes were often lost or complicated by political agendas. He said he had returned to Port Moresby because there is no work and 'too much fighting'.

Peter Donigi, the Papua New Guinea United Nations (UN) representative, said it is not the system of government or its laws that is undermining good governance, but the choice of people in senior posts and political interference in administrating the public sector. He suggested amendments to the Constitution that limits parliamentary members holding executive positions, the introduction of a Code of Ethics to bind all government delegates, and a change of the first-past-the-post voting system to optional preferential voting (1998). Former Prime Minister, Sir Rabbie Namaliu, painted a gloomy picture of the lack of anti-corruption initiatives, and the incapacity of the government and its law and order agencies to prosecute and punish offenders. He said while massive scandals involving state-owned corporations and institutions had been uncovered with losses exceeding K500 million over the past five years, no one had been or would be prosecuted or made to repay the money. Sir Rabbie called for an independent prosecutor to prepare charges against alleged defrauders, and set up a permanent Independent Anti-Corruption Commission to restore public confidence in government (*Post-Courier* 23 October 2000:3). However, at the AusAID-funded PNG Economic Update in Port Moresby on 25 October 2001, an amnesty for past corruption was strongly advocated to ensure parliament passed legislation to form an Independent Commission Against Corruption. The view was that parliament would not pass the Act without an amnesty, as 'half [of its members] would go to jail' (Ame 2001:4).

Throughout this book I build on the arguments and views of Clifford, Morauta and Stuart (1984a and b) and Dinnen (1992, 1994a, 1994b, 1998, 1999, 2000) and others, that community controls are more effective than state controls. I guide the reader through anecdotal and factual data to show the relationship between politics, leadership, accountability, corruption and capacity—within and between state agencies and local communities—that often stymies both state and community crime control initiatives.

In Chapters 1 and 2, I set the scene in which crime flourishes, exploring its status within historical, demographic, political, social and economic contexts. In Chapter 3, I consider the status of crime in Papua New Guinea, the available statistics, and overview the influences, demands and deficiencies of state agencies that hamper their efforts to prevent and control crime. In Chapter 4, I consider the impact of resource deficiencies, policy development and donor funded institutional strengthening inputs. In Chapter 5, I discuss links between communities and criminal justice agencies to prevent and control crime, and highlight the difficulties of sustaining initiatives. In Chapter 6, I argue that, until adequate and consistent resource levels are maintained to implement initiatives, regulate leaders, and prosecute and punish public defrauders, all efforts to control crime by either governments or communities will fail. In Chapter 7, I reiterate the link between leadership integrity, resource availability, and the consequences of weak, corrupt regimes that do not provide for citizens, do not involve them in decision making and do not keep them informed—rendering crime control and other initiatives impotent.

Note

1 'Payback' is a violent revengeful act that pays back a person or his or her family for a grievance.

1 The historical, demographic and socio-economic complexity of crime and crime control

Traders and explorers from Asia and Europe had either been to or had known of Papua New Guinea for centuries. While some developed trade networks, others exploited coastal communities for their rich natural resources and labour. As in other Pacific island countries, traders and missionaries paved the way for colonists. Missionaries were not far behind the wave of European prospectors and traders who had been visiting Papua New Guinea since the 1830s. Papua became a protectorate of Britain in 1884 and a colony known as British New Guinea in 1888. At the same time, the German Government vested administrative control of New Guinea in a German trading company (Firth 1986).

Pre-colonial Papua New Guinea has a long and exotic history. It is believed that man has lived there for up to fifty thousand years—today's people descendants of successive waves of migration from Asia. When the colonisers arrived the indigenous population boasted more than 700 languages belonging to two major language groups: Austronesian and Non-Austronesian. The former live in the mainland hinterland and hills; the latter occupy the coasts and islands (Waiko 1993). Traditional PNG societies comprised of local descent groups, have complex social structures and live in villages, hamlets or dispersed homesteads. The societies are spread over 462,840 square kilometres of either very fertile or very rugged customary owned land and 1,900,000 square kilometres of customary owned sea. Prior to colonial contact, many inland groups were isolated from frequent external contact by language and geography. Periodic contact did occur nevertheless, and a series of elaborate trade and political alliance networks developed over thousands of years.

Trade in some PNG island communities was vigorous and expansive. Traders, whalers and passenger vessels travelling to and from Australia participated and some island trade networks extended to Southeast Asia and New Caledonia. Goods traded included fruit, vegetables, salt, sago, fish, obsidian (a glass-like volcanic rock used for tools and weapons), pottery, ceremonial shells, bird of paradise feathers, and stone axe blades. The networks facilitated exchange of ideas and attitudes as well as the exchange of goods. Reciprocity bound groups and fostered reconciliation (Waiko 1993, Hunt 1998). There was also vigorous trade between highlands and coastal communities, and well-trodden trade routes criss-crossed the country. Archaeological evidence suggests that some highlands communities like the Kuk people of the Western Highlands Province, were amongst the world's first agriculturalists. Nine thousand years ago they grew bananas, pitpit, green vegetables and possibly sugar cane. They had sophisticated agricultural and drainage systems and kept domesticated animals. In the PNG highlands, trade networks included the *tee* exchange of pigs and other valuables among Engans, *moka-making* in the Wahgi Valley by the Melpa people, and the *mok ink* in the Mendi region of the Southern Highlands. More recent coastal arrivals 5,000 years ago developed elaborate seaborne trading systems like the *Hiri,* between the Motu people of Port Moresby and Gulf Province peoples to the west, and the *Kula* ring linking south-east mainland Papua to the Trobriand Islands and the Louisiade Archipelago (Griffin et al. 1979).

Social and economic organisation was and still is governed by flexible networks of kinship relations. Complex social relationships and ceremonial practices reflect the relationship of the people to the physical environment and to the history of their societies. PNG societies comprise nuclear and extended families within a group of clans whose membership is based on kinship through blood, marriage or adoption (Waiko 1993).

Prior to colonisation, land was subject to customary tenure. Ninety-five per cent of land in Papua New Guinea is still customary owned—distributed through kinship relations and social relationships upon which traditional value systems are based. Tenure is dynamic and governed by land usage. Individual and group needs and wants at a given time result in constant negotiations at community level regarding temporary or permanent access to and use of land (Hunt 1998).

Traditional political leaders in PNG societies may be either 'big men' who achieve power through physical and intellectual ability or material wealth, or hereditary chiefs. Leaders are expected to negotiate relationships, distribute wealth, and arbitrate disputes. Hereditary chieftainships are found in some coastal areas and islands. Chiefs usually inherit their title from their fathers and are part of a rigid hierarchical social structure. Exceptions to these lineages can be found in some societies on the Gazelle Peninsula, where ancestors are traced through females and land rights are transmitted from mother to daughter. Core disputes in pre-contact Papua New Guinea were over land or women. Disputes were resolved and societies regulated by swift and sometimes harsh punishment. Tribal fighting was a frequent form of dispute resolution, played out according to traditionally recognised rules (Waiko 1993). Wounding, death, and destruction of gardens, houses and livestock resulted in payback killings, payback destruction, payback sorcery, compensation or combinations of all four. Carefully planned and orchestrated compensation ceremonies were and still are the most effective dispute resolution strategy.

Adultery and desertion in many PNG societies are considered to be on a par with or worse than murder and often women, rather than men are penalised. Traditional penalties in some communities were harsh and included the amputation of feet, mutilation of sexual organs or stoning. Other disputes were and still are resolved through community leaders and elders who arbitrate a settlement between aggrieved parties. This settlement usually comprises compensation.

Traditionally, compensation consisted of live pigs and pig meat, vegetables and other produce, ceremonial items like bird of paradise feathers, shells and other goods. It remains common for disputes to be settled in this way but large sums of money and vehicles are now included.

Papua New Guinea colonised

Into these complex and participatory societies, where attention to detail and lengthy liaison achieved conciliatory outcomes, the British New Guinea administration introduced a magisterial system of an armed indigenous constabulary and village constables to maintain a Western style of order. Commissioned officers, all white men called *kiaps* (TP: patrol officers) played several roles including policemen, explorer, road builder, health inspector, social worker, prison warder, census officer, linguist and historian. They arbitrated grievances—acting as prosecutor, defence counsel, judge and jury—and conducted patrols to remote locations providing basic services, checking populations and health conditions and introducing regulations and policies according to assessment of the readiness of an area for development. The colonial administrator, William MacGregor, introduced 'native regulations'. The regulations were aimed at civilising Papuan communities by outlawing practices like sorcery, adultery, assault, theft, spreading 'lying reports', and destruction of 'valuable' trees. Village constables were installed to arbitrate disputes. They were not always local leaders or elders however and lacked 'traditional' authority.

The German New Guinea administrator, Albert Hahl, utilised traditional leadership systems to maintain order at local levels. He initiated a *Luluai* system as a form of indirect rule at village level. Village leaders were appointed as village constables called *Luluai* (from the Kuanua language *lualua* connoting headship). They were assisted by *Tultuls* (another Kuanua term) who often acted as interpreters. *Luluai* powers were severely limited subsequently and they became mere administrative officers allowed only to regulate disputes relating to money, garden produce and animals, to punish people with cash fines, to keep village order, to oversee road building, disease control and village agriculture, and to collect head tax. They were barred from granting divorces, hearing land disputes, or disputes over territorial boundaries, tribal fighting, murders, burglaries, property damage, incest, rape, or adultery. This restricted role undermined the potency of their traditional leadership. The German Annual Report of 1901 records the *Luluai* system as unsuccessful because *Luluai* were not prepared to give up their positions of power to become loyal to a foreign authority.

In 1901 Britain transferred British New Guinea to Australia and in 1919, after the Treaty of Versailles, Australia was given a mandate to administer the former colony of German New Guinea. *Luluai* were further disempowered in the early years of the Australian regime, losing their judicial function and ceasing to arbitrate minor disputes (Chalmers 1978, Wolfers 1975). By 1927, however, the Australians were realising the importance of fostering traditional institutions and tribunals and of encouraging traditional leaders to take a more active role in managing their affairs. In the new Territory of Papua and New Guinea *Luluai* regained their power and for thirty years were valuable intermediaries between Government and communities. During this time there were two major population dispersals that brought new ideas, systems, and goods to remote regions. One occurred in response to plantation industry expansion, the other in response to new systems of government. From the 1920s, labourers for plantations in Papua, East and West New Britain, New Ireland, and various parts of the New Guinea mainland was recruited and indentured for one or two years, then sent home. Some returned to work on the same or other plantations after a home stay. The biggest plantation recruitments occurred from poorer regions like the East Sepik and Gulf Provinces, and later from the Southern Highlands and Simbu Provinces. In 1980 I visited an elderly Englishman on his plantation at Abau in eastern Papua. He told me he used to go 'black birding up the Fly' (Fly River) and was often attacked by warriors with spears. One 'black birder', he said, was eaten. The mobilisation of indigenous police constables, prison officers, teachers, health workers and missionaries, increased the knowledge and understanding of local peoples in relation to the colonial regime and worlds beyond. Policemen in particular played a front-line role in maintaining local order, imposing their will by playing politics, forming tactical marriage alliances and being aggressive and enthusiastic agents of change. Many PNG citizens today are of mixed parentage—their mothers or fathers, posted to other provinces, having married locally or married other posted workers.

The change in attitude to colonisation after World War II brought freedom to many indigenous peoples or at least, greater participation in the economy and government. The Australian administrator of the Territory of Papua and New Guinea, J.K. Murray, was an advocate of such change. He was an active administrator respected by the indigenous population, who rode on horseback over great distances to check difficult situations or participate in events. In the late 1940s he convinced Australia that native village courts were needed to deal with minor civil and criminal matters, particularly those relating to custom. This led to the passing of the *Papua and New Guinea Act* in 1949. By the late 1950s there was a stronger push by the Western world to liberate people subject to draconian colonial regimes under 'dual' systems of law. Dual systems have one law for colonialists and one law for indigenes. The new Minister for Territories, Paul Hasluck, opposed the dual village court and Western court system in the Territory of Papua New Guinea appointing Professor David Derham of Melbourne University to review the administration of justice and prepare a report. The 1960 Derham Report provided the basis for the system of law enforcement and judicial administration for the new state of Papua New Guinea. The report advocated the gradual dismantling of district administrations and the establishment of clear divisions of labour between the police, the judiciary, and the prison service. In 1961 the police force was separated from the Department of Native Affairs and by 1966 removed from the direct control of the Public Service Commission. In 1963 in accordance with Derham's recommendations and with a view to 'civilising' the indigenous inhabitants, the Westminster legal system of Local, District and Supreme Courts was introduced. In the same year the Native Customs Recognition Ordinance was passed to increase accessibility of villagers to the new legal system and to create fairness in sentencing.

local level government (LLG) councils were appointed in each area to enable people to administer their own affairs in accordance with the law, while *Luluai* lost their powers to the newly appointed councillors. However, unlike the village court system, councillors appointed under the Westminster system had no judicial power to arbitrate offences against either traditional or modern laws. In 1968 most native regulations enforced by *kiaps* were repealed and replaced by summary offences codified in modern criminal statutes. These changes broke the link between custom and administration, forced reversion to modified forms of customary law and undermined local social controls. The new laws were not considered just. This is because Melanesian justice requires compensation to either the victim or the victim's group. Unlike *kiap* law, which used a wide range of sentencing options, was direct, and made decisions quickly, new law magistrates were restricted to certain judgements, failed to consider local dispute resolution needs and took longer to make decisions. There was a need for a mechanism that incorporated the positive elements of 'custom' in local dispute resolution. In response, the 1973 *Village Court Act* was passed. To maximise co-operation, village courts were established according to traditional political alliances and local magistrates were appointed, recommended by provincial magistrates in consultation with LLG councils.

The Derham Report, the Native Customs Recognition Ordinance, and Village Court Acts lacked understanding of the value of compensation to reconcile differences. Moreover the reality is that an offence under Westminster law is not necessarily an offence under customary law. For these reasons PNG communities today remain detached from state law, and state law remains limited in its application. For example, in relation to the Native Customs Recognition Ordinance, custom could only be taken into account for particular purposes in criminal cases. In relation to the establishment of village courts according to traditional political alliances, alliances change from time to time according to need and dispute. Also the socio-economic effects of colonisation were breaking down traditional power structures and alliances. This was because of new wealth gained from access to the colonial regime, Western education, in and out migration, and intermarriage across regions.

Some individuals and communities did and still do benefit from their association with the State. For example, it is considered prestigious by LLG councillors and village court magistrates to be 'servants' of the State. This is because access to *kago* (goods and services) including western education for their children is more assured. At the same time, individuals can maintain a modified 'traditional' place through local level government council or village court magistrate election and thereby have 'a leg in each camp'. This situation benefits both the interests of local level government and the State as long as the State continues to inject information and provide goods and services. Under the colonial regime, *kiaps* conducted foot patrols to remote areas providing information and services from the external world. They worked with village constables to implement a degree of social control—providing an intermediary function and legitimating customary law—resulting in positive dispute resolution. Some communities resented *kiap* administration, perceiving *kiaps* to be racist and lazy. Moreover the 1960 Derham report argued that *kiaps* who were not trained as legal practitioners and had insufficient knowledge to dispense justice adequately. The late Christopher Waite who worked as a *kiap* in the 1950s told me 'We had to prove ourselves. Everyone was watching us and we had to be strong and follow through our promises to maintain their [the community's] confidence and we had to remain neutral'. Both government and communities expected much of *kiaps*. They were to perform in the field after only six months' training with no prior knowledge of the country. Most were young and inexperienced. Chris, who had his twenty-first birthday in Port Moresby shortly after his arrival, said he relied heavily on his indigenous sergeant for advice, support, and for education in language, local customs and beliefs.

While *kiap* administration did not always achieve its ends, it was designed to administer local communities with a mixture of reward and punishment as part of which compensation ceremonies were sanctioned. *Kiap* courts provided additional forums incorporating local political strategies and at the same time, reinforcing state law. With the phasing out of the *kiap* system there was a gradual withdrawal of information, goods and services. Many citizens considered the new regime to be weak, believing that provincial government delegates lacked neutrality and communities did not understand the new laws. Tribal fighting re-emerged in the early 1970s with the gradual withdrawal of *kiaps*. With a view to containing and ultimately extinguishing tribal fighting, the 1997 *Inter-Group Fighting Act* was passed, criminalising participation in it. However neither the Act nor the incarceration of individuals and groups has stopped the fighting and spasmodic, destructive flare-ups continue in the highlands. In 1981, while travelling with and acting as scribe for the Electoral Boundaries Commission, I recorded a Pogera district elder saying 'The *kiaps* did not take sides in fights. They were strong and fair and we usually stopped the fight. They also walked many miles to see us to bring us *kago* and tell us of the outside world'. In 1997 and 1999, while visiting prisons and provincial governments and participating in public forums, I listened to complaints to provincial administrators that communities had been excluded from goods, services, information and arbitration since the withdrawal of the *kiaps*. For example, at a community meeting on the jetty at Ambunti on the Sepik River in May 1997, local level government councillors complained that neither the police nor provincial welfare and community development officers visited remote communities on foot 'like the *kiaps* did'. In terms of social control, the withdrawal of *kiaps* without replacing them with a similar, popular, adequately resourced system, resulted in a perception by local communities that the State could no longer provide goods and services for their advancement or protection. This perception consolidated an insularity of thinking and action which has not only resulted in continued sporadic tribal fighting but also permeates the decisions and actions of provincial governments, LLG councils and village courts. Political fragmentation spread, reinforced by the State's incapacity to provide goods and services. It began as a result of Derham Report recommendations to decentralise the Colonial Government before a national identity could be achieved. The cumulative effect of the changes over a long period of time, and especially during the post-Independence period, undermined the credibility of a centralised state (Dinnen 1998).

In 1962 colonial Papua New Guinea was thrust onto the world stage by United Nations' criticism of the lack of political development.

The United Nations advocated the establishment of a House of Assembly and the development of higher education to train indigenes for senior positions in the bureaucracy. Many indigenes and foreigners thought self-government was too soon as neither a national identity nor a 'home grown' constitution had been developed. There was no quelling the United Nations' determination however and Australia made concerted attempts to create an 'instant' democracy with a national identity. As part of this effort, a House of Assembly made up of educated indigenes and foreigners was elected. With a view to breaking down ethnic barriers and creating national unity, many Papua and New Guinean adolescents were sent to high school in different parts of the country. For example, Papuans went to school in Goroka, Gorokans went to school in Lae, Lae youth went to school in Rabaul, Madang youth went to school in Wewak. Others gained scholarships to schools and colleges in Australia. A PNG woman told me 'We girls were sent to the Blue Mountains when we were fourteen or fifteen and stayed there until we were eighteen or nineteen. Some of us didn't come back. Those of us who did were very changed'. The experiment, together with ensuing cross-cultural marriages, broke down traditional ethnic barriers but created others. Friendships were formed from the new social networks and sub-cultures of ethnically bonded people through school and work. These broadened alliances are utilised actively, the more astute players blending 'traditional' and modern expectations to achieve political and economic objectives.

Abolition of restrictions on indigenous social movement accelerated migration into towns in the 1960s. Some migrants were 'pulled' to town to seek adventure, excitement and material gain, while others were 'pushed' from their communities to escape a commitment at home. These commitments included marriage and compensation demands or may have involved physical danger resulting from a dispute. Those 'pulled' to town remained uneducated, unskilled and unemployed. From the early 1970s, the Central Planning Office was raising concerns about the growing gap between the number of youth joining the labour market and diminishing access to education beyond grade six. State capacity was already limited to support a formal wage structure and private sector employment had begun to stagnate.

Despite this, in 1974 the Minimum Wages Board institutionalised the Australian practice of 'indexation' and established six-monthly automatic cost-of-living minimum wage adjustments. This resulted in an inappropriate and inflexible wages policy—detrimental to economic growth and development. The weekly urban wage for regulated employment rose to K25.80. In contrast, rural wages remained at only K1.00 per week plus payment in kind and a 12.5 per cent loading. By 1975 the gap between rural and urban wages had risen, encouraging further migration. But the growing urban populace faced decreased job opportunities due to economic stagnation, and at Independence, only half of urban dwellers were employed. Thus the foundation was laid for urban underemployment and a massive crime wave. Over the next twenty-five years the private sector stagnated further, the labour market shrank, and the urban population increased four-fold, driving many people to 'informal' activities including unregistered family businesses, crime, prostitution, street vending, casual labouring, bottle collection and work as 'security guards' (Levantis and Fane 1997).

The rapid influx of migrants into urban centres in the 1960s and 1970s began to cause social problems. Some urban migrants behaved badly in Port Moresby—spending their money on women, drink and gambling because they believed 'town' offered no real social controls and sanctions (Strathern 1977). Criminal gangs called 'hooligans', then 'rascals', began causing problems in settlements in Port Moresby where, in the 1960s and 1970s, some thirteen gangs were operating. Disillusionment forced young, unskilled and unemployed male migrants to form peer groups evolving into criminal gangs. Criminal hierarchy was structured along 'traditional' lines with members supporting the goals of leaders in return for sustenance. Criminal acts were condoned and encouraged within a framework of cooperation and mutual support, each member possessing the right to share the 'bounty'. In contrast with these 'traditional' cooperatives, the new urban indigenous élite had become heavily reliant on the state legal system for protection. The chasm between rich and poor grew and under-achievers, engaged in criminality, were further victimised and alienated. Conflicts were increasing between traditional and modern thinking, the old and young, Western educated and uneducated, rich and poor, urban and rural (Harris 1998).

As perceptions changed so did expectations. Power bases shifted due to education, Western wealth, intermarriage, and general exposure to the external world. Change caused uncertainties and conflicts and increased traditional social tensions over land, women and power. In terms of social control, the colonial legacy to post-independent Papua New Guinea was weak, fragmented, inappropriate and inadequate. The political and legal systems were managed by a mere one per cent of the population. Thus the recommendations of the 1960 Derham Report, though well meaning, were premature and modelled on Western history, philosophy and a morality alien to many Papua New Guineans. No national identity and no written history had, at that time, been created and no unity of national tradition had been experienced. Centralised law enforcement and judicial administration undermined state power at community levels, forcing people to revert to their own more understandable methods of crime control. At the same time, citizens were denied the political and socio-economic benefits of blending local customs with democratic philosophy and law to resolve disputes and to access resources.

Moral power that could have been derived from locally-developed policy, was lost due to the centralised government's top-down administration that did not reflect the concerns and values of communities. People felt alienated from government process and policy, and government initiatives were and continue to be sabotaged by non-cooperation or other measures. These forces that drove political, social and economic fragmentation are the reasons why Papua New Guinea was a weak, politically fragmented state at the time of independence. Colonialists, the international human rights community and the indigenous élite were carried on a wave of idealistic optimism of the potential of the new nation state of Papua New Guinea. The reality was a rapidly expanding population of 2,185,000 with 700 languages—trapped in pockets of isolation from social and economic advancement by rugged and impassable physical terrain—and trapped in a social and economic environment of illiteracy, scant information, and inadequate goods and services. The expectations of the ability of the educated elite to administer and participate in recently learned foreign, legal and bureaucratic systems and foreign politics were unrealistically high. Expectations that the foreign legal system could accommodate the needs of PNG citizens for expression, reward, punishment and restitution, were likewise misguided. In the mid 1970s concerns were expressed regarding rapidly rising crime in urban areas. Forums were held, policies recommended and strategies devised. On 14 August 1974 a Peace and Good Order Committee was set up to investigate the status of crime and on 8 March 1975, the Chief Minister, Michael Somare, telexed the Australian Attorney-General, Mr Enderby, that there is 'serious and mounting concern (regarding crime)...(no) coordinated Government plan to deal with (its) control and prevention of crime' (Clifford 1976:4–6). The Chief Minister asked William Clifford to visit Papua New Guinea to investigate the situation.

Post-independence Papua New Guinea

On 16 September 1975 the new nation state of Papua New Guinea became a constitutional democracy with a free press. One hundred and nine members of parliament represented 20 provinces including the National Capital District and 89 districts. Ninety-seven per cent of the land was customary owned and over 85 per cent of the population lived in rural areas in subsistence or semi-subsistence. The new nation state was very much a colonial creation. Australian aid constituted 40 per cent of the PNG National Budget and approximately 30,000 expatriates, mainly Australians, resided in the country working in government and private enterprise. Most Papua New Guineans did not attend school and few advanced past sixth grade. Less than five years prior to Independence only 0.1 per cent (approximately 2,500) of the population had reached high school (Harden 1999:ii), and at Independence this small, educated élite was expected to administer government through political candidature and senior line management public service roles in an over-bureaucratised public service set in an environment with an underclass of illiterate urban and rural communities.

The over-bureaucratised, democratic administration and Westminster legal system—developed in ancient nation states with long written histories—did not suit the oral society of Papua New Guinea that was ethnically, culturally and politically diverse. Political fragmentation began to occur, reinforced by tensions between provincial and national politicians and the reversion of communities to social controls sanctioned by small-scale political entities that characterised pre-colonial Papua New Guinea. From 1977, shifts in coalitions have caused every parliament to change mid-term, diminishing the State's ability to deliver goods and services and to commit to long-term policy—an ideal climate for corruption and nepotism (May 1998). In 1977 the indigenous population of Port Moresby was 95,000 but one-quarter of the adult male population did not have legitimate work. In the 1980s only 4,000 formal jobs were created each year yet the labour force was increasing by 40,000 a year. Only one in ten people was expected to find work and it was estimated in 1980, that over 52 per cent of youth under the age of 25 years had no education (O'Connell and Zarriga 1991:214–5). Not surprisingly, between 1975 and 1980, 20 rascal gangs were operating in the city (Garnaut 1979:5–6, Harris 1998:42). At the same time, corruption was escalating in government circles and initial attempts to prosecute offenders failed. Law and order was deteriorating and the economy was stagnant. The Ombudsman Commission was inundated with allegations of fraud, bribery, nepotism and other corrupt practice relating to the awarding of contracts, business liaisons and administration of government funds.

Two major studies, the Morgan Report (1983) and the Clifford Report (1984), were commissioned to recommend realistic strategies to curb crime and build investor confidence. The Morgan Report reviewed policy and administration while the Clifford Report produced a comprehensive list of recommendations observing that law and order problems in Papua New Guinea were to a large extent, political problems that manifested in poor relations between the State and its citizens. Such problems were aggravated by corruption and became the focus of manoeuvres and conflict between government agencies. The Clifford Report estimated that in 1984 only 20 per cent of all crimes were reported to the police: an indication that communities had lost faith in government either to protect them or to provide basic goods and services (Clifford 1984:iii,15, Clifford, Morauta and Stuart 1984a). Tribal fighting and other traditional dispute resolution strategies continued to provide partial solutions to unresolvable law and order problems in some highlands regions. Bureaucratic stagnancy and community detachment from state laws prompted Clifford to recommend to the National Executive Council that a new law and order policy be adopted that charged informal and community institutions with the maintenance of order, and recommended the provision of state resources to compliment and support informal institutions.

Population growth, literacy, health, unemployment and crime

Population growth

Papua New Guinea's exploding youth population, stagnant formal employment, low literacy and poor health services created an environment that encouraged serious and frequent crime. Between 1966 and 1990 the population increased by almost 1.6 million. In 1990 the population was estimated at 4 million; in 2000 it was 5.1 million and 25 years after Independence, 88 per cent of the PNG population is estimated to live in rural areas,[1] unemployed, or involved in subsistence agriculture or smallholder cash cropping. Forty-one per cent of the rural population was estimated to be 'poor and uneducated' with inadequate or no access to basic services and highly vulnerable to natural disasters and negative external shocks (National Statistical Office 2001:11–32, World Bank 1999:vii,75).

In 1998 the United Nations Population Fund (UNFPA) predicted an annual youth population increase of 30,000 per year by 2020 if the PNG birth rate remains unchanged and estimated that the labour force needs to grow by four per cent per annum for the next 20 years to absorb those coming into it (*The National* 9 July 1998:16). Presently, PNG's annual economic growth averages only 1.1 per centper capita. In 2000 there were almost one million young people between the ages of 15 and 24 years in Papua New Guinea, many unemployed. Port Moresby has one of the world's worst crime rates and one of the world's highest unemployment rates. By 2015 the NCD population is expected to increase by 2.7 times its 1990 level. Given that almost 55 per cent of the NCD population are males, that mainly young men in the 15 to 24-year age group commit crime, and that Papua New Guinea's annual economic growth rate will not generate enough employment for this group, crime will continue to escalate. Already the NCD population has outstripped the capacity of the city authority to provide reliable electricity and telecommunications, there are frequent telephone disconnections and rolling electricity cuts. Businesses, which could generate employment, have difficulty surviving and new investors—and potential employers—do not want to waste their time and risk their money in an environment with inefficient utilities, where their property and personal rights are not protected, where they are compelled to pay bribes to corrupt officials to keep the telephones and electricity on, and where they are further hampered from conducting business by the threat of robberies and muggings.

Literacy

Feelings of worthlessness caused by having no employment and no legitimate avenue of advancement is a precondition of criminality. In 1990 only half of PNG children between 10 and 14 years attended school, only 23 per cent of 15 and 19-year olds were enrolled and only three per cent accessed tertiary institutions (National Statistical Office 1995:16). In other words, while 80 per cent of children receive some primary school education, only 14 per cent enrol in secondary schools. Compared with Fiji, Thailand, East Asia and low–middle income countries, Papua New Guinea has the lowest school enrolments at either level. As a result, only 45 per cent of the adult population is literate and the country has the second lowest literacy rate in the Pacific (Office of National Planning 1999b:12). Moreover the National Statistical Office (1995:18) reported that an average of only 29 per cent of the estimated average of 45 per cent 'total literate' were literate in English.

There are high attrition rates in schools especially in lower grades. Causes include English language difficulties, unavailability of certain grades at some schools, insufficient school places in existing grades, poor quality education, inappropriate curricula and the inability of poor households to pay education costs. Almost half the children who obtain any formal education in Papua New Guinea attend vocational schools. These schools provide valuable artisanal training, making them more attractive to employers. There are insufficient places in vocational schools to accommodate all those who need them and even if there were, existing curricula for rural students is not designed for rural self-employment beyond subsistence agriculture; basic workshop or handicraft skills like woodwork and metalwork or how to change tap washers are rarely taught. This deficiency may relate to a lack of resources to support such education.

Adult male prisoners express frustration and feelings of neglect in relation to their experience of, or minimal access to, formal education. Those who have attended school say 'school was a waste of time and didn't teach us anything'. Others who have not attended school may make up for it in prison by studying through the College of Distance Education (CODE) if they or their families can afford the fees. They say that if they had access to the CODE previously they 'would not be in prison now as they would have been able to get a good job'. One male ex-prisoner told me in May 1999 'I don't understand a lot of things because I didn't go to school. I just listen to people and pick things up. But I get very confused and then I get angry and I just want to do crazy things'. All but one of the 16 and 17-year old juvenile male prisoners in Bomana jail in April 1998 had not been to school. One had tried it for a few months and left. The parents of others did not have money for school fees or another sibling had gone to school instead. One had lived on the streets since he was nine because his mother's new husband did not want him. All wanted to learn to read and write so they could 'get jobs'. At the Badili City Mission in Port Moresby some youths 'study CODE' that is, study through the School of Distance Education. Other residents want to learn to read and write, 'to get a good job' so they can 'be someone' and 'help my family'. Some want to learn work skills 'to make things to sell'. They are not able to go to vocational schools however because 'you have to have grade six' and because there is 'no money to pay school fees'.

Health

Papua New Guinea has more health centres than Indonesia and China. Its infant and maternal mortality rates however are the highest and its life expectancy is the lowest of lower–middle-income countries and in East Asia and the Pacific. In 1998, 88 per cent of PNG citizens appeared to have access to health services. Real accessibility however is governed by the amount of cash people have to pay for services, the capacity of the Department of Health to maintain services, and the status of infrastructure. At Independence, Papua New Guinea had a three-tier community-based health care system adequate and appropriate for the country's needs. Since Independence, the physical infrastructure has deteriorated due to minimal operational funds, breakdown of supervision and referral, and unclear divisions of responsibilities between local and provincial governments. In 1996 only 39 per cent of health facilities were in satisfactory condition; in 2001 less than 70 per cent of rural aid posts were operating.

Another serious indictment of the inadequate health system is the rise of HIV/AIDS. The National Department of Health believes HIV infection is at epidemic proportions and that for every case detected, 10 more go undetected. This suggests that an estimated 0.5 per cent of the population are infected. A report released in 2001 by the National AIDS Council estimated that 10,000–15,000 PNG citizens are infected with the HIV virus. The number of newly detected HIV/AIDS cases—64 per cent of which are in the National Capital District and 32 per cent in Highlands provinces—continues to rise. Twenty-four per cent of those diagnosed are 'unemployed' and 21 per cent are 'housewives' (*The National* 13 March 2001). The high incidence of sexual violence towards women is believed to be a major contributor to the spread of HIV infection. In 1998, 1,513 serious sexual offences were reported. Papua New Guinea ranks second in the world for sexual violence against women, rape and pack-rape being common, while 40 per cent of (reported) rape victims are young girls (RPNGC 1998, *The National* 15 March 1999:4).

HIV/AIDS awareness programs in jails, schools, communities, amongst police and other public servants have so far failed to reduce the rate of infection. While the Catholic Church and other non-government organisations work hard to provide information and assistance, awareness amongst provincial health workers is low. Some churches preach bigoted doctrines regarding sexual relationships that put ill-informed parishioners at risk, advocating morality rather than harm minimisation, condemning condom distribution and distorting valuable information from the Department of Health on HIV virus contraction. In early 2000 stickers for sale at a stand outside the Port Moresby post office stated, 'Adultery is sin more worse than aids virus'. To compound this bigotry and bias, diagnostic capacity is inadequate, counselling and care of HIV infected persons and AIDS patients and their families is minimal, and sexual behaviour remains a sensitive topic defeating efforts to minimise harm. Unless the government makes a concerted effort to pay health workers regularly, educate and train practitioners and citizens and support harm minimisation strategies, AIDS will kill more people, cripple families and communities and impair the economy severely.

The Port Moresby population is heavily dependent upon health services. But frustrations flare into aggressive attacks upon health clinic staff and facilities when people, who bring their sick relatives to clinics are 'turned away with an aspirin, because there is insufficient time to see them, no drugs to treat them, no doctor is available or the clinic is closed. In November 1999, the Gordons Health Clinic in Port Moresby, which serviced some 8,000 people (200 patients a day), closed due to a crack in the building's foundation causing flooding and rendering it uninhabitable. As a result, client pressure doubled on the next closest health clinic at Six Mile. In June 2000 there were only seven health clinics operating in Port Moresby, each with limited capacity to service the client population.

In 2001, the Gordons Health Clinic remained closed. Poor diets, poor sanitation and minimal access to potable water cause frequent illness and premature death. This causes panic and frustration in communities and often leads to criminality. Fights occur over scarce resources, and low or no income earners resort to crime to get cash to pay health service fees, for transport to clinics and hospitals, or for frequent funeral expenses. In Port Moresby urban villages sanitation is poor, rubbish disposal infrequent, access to garden land scarce and there is a reliance on high sugar, fatty and salty foods. The consumption of such foods has increased obesity, heart disease and diabetes. Poor nutrition is linked with crime. Studies in the United States and Australia indicate a strong link between deficiencies of Vitamin B and aggressive mood swings manifesting in aberrant behaviour (Kirschmann and Kirschmann 1996). In low-income rural and urban PNG households it is common for children to eat last, in meagre proportions, not more than once a day and sometimes less. Children with inadequate diets do not concentrate well and their ability to absorb information is reduced. When this occurs parents may withdraw them from school and replace them with siblings who are more likely academic achievers. Health statistics indicate that 62 per cent of PNG children between 24–35 months are stunted. This means that unless their diet improves they will grow into poorly nourished youth who may suffer learning difficulties and behavioural problems, and then drop out of school to potentially join criminal gangs and terrorise communities.

In 1999 in Port Moresby alone, it was estimated that over one-quarter of the population was poor with minimal access to income, food, and other goods and services. It was also estimated that nationally over 37 per cent of the population was below the poverty line—the poverty line is defined as the cost of a food consumption basket that meets a minimum food-energy requirement of 2,200 calories per adult equivalent per day. A 1996 poverty assessment in Papua New Guinea found that the National Capital District had the lowest calorie consumption in the country, a reason being that people do not have the means to produce food or the money to purchase an adequate supply (United Nations Development Programme [UNDP] 1999:86, Gibson and Rozelle 1998, World Bank 1999). As youth access to food, formal education and employment shrinks their vulnerability and desperateness to eat, 'be someone', 'look smart', and 'make money' reinforces the legitimacy of their criminal actions.

Unemployment and crime

High urban youth unemployment is linked with a high incidence of crime, undermining investment, economic growth and development. Young males, with no money and nothing to do, seek targets for theft and aggression. Armed robberies, assaults, breaking and entering, carjacking, bag snatching and pick pocketing result. In 1990 the urban unemployed comprised 82 per cent of 10–14-year olds, 63 per cent of 15–19-year olds and 35 per cent of 20–24-year olds. In 2001, in Port Moresby, 60 per cent of the population was jobless (National Statistical Office 1995:23, *Post-Courier* 12 September 2001:1–5). In 1999 the workforce grew by almost two per cent outstripping the economy's capacity to create jobs. There are several reasons why only a small proportion of the 20,000 young people who reach workforce age each year are absorbed into formal employment. First, the demand is for skilled workers—those with little or no education or specific skills are precluded. Second, wage employment has contracted due to a lack of investor confidence. Third, there are substantial differences between rural and urban incomes.

Youth absorption into formal employment is a major economic challenge for Papua New Guinea. In lieu of legitimate jobs and educational opportunities, and with a view to building self-esteem and allaying deprivation, considerable numbers of children and youth are drawn into the crime industry. Serious crime has been growing at four per cent a year since 1990. In that year, 80 per cent of the 'unemployed' had left school at grade six or before, 35 per cent had no formal education and 150,000 people were unemployed (National Statistical Office 1995:21–3). Almost 66,000 'unemployed' persons live in urban areas. In a 1995 survey of 337 people in Port Moresby, it was discovered that 69.2 per cent of males who considered themselves 'unemployed' were 'employed' in criminal activities, their earnings from such illicit activity equating to 'the relatively high wages of unskilled labour in the formal sector'. Significantly, the survey revealed that criminality offers unskilled youth more earning potential than formal, unskilled labour. Because of this, few 'unemployed' youth actively seek formal, skilled employment (Levantis 1997). Survey findings concur with the view of Bomana prisoners that if they had access to formal education they 'would not be in prison now as they would have been able to get a good job'.

In Papua New Guinea, women fare worse than men, most are less educated than men and thus have fewer formal employment opportunities. In 1990 more males than females continued formal education after the age of 15 (National Statistical Office 1995:16). The same applies today. Many 'unemployed' women work as prostitutes—*pulim man* (TP: enticing men to have sex that is, low-scale and irregular prostitution)—to meet financial obligations. In 1995 it was found that a staggering 38.3 per cent of females who said they were 'unemployed' were participating in prostitution (Levantis 1997:77). Others sell marihuana to feed their families and meet other obligations. Between January and June 1998 all but two women prisoners at Bomana prison had been sentenced to three and six months imprisonment for prostitution. Most were married with children.

A woman whom I shall call 'Mona' told me that when she first came to Port Moresby with small children she dabbled in prostitution. She had been prevented from going to school, her marriage had been arranged with an unskilled labourer and she had lost her economic independence in the urban setting. Her husband's income did not support the family. There were already three children and the ground was too arid in the urban settlement where they lived to grow vegetables. The cost of living was high and there were still *wantok* (TP: traditionally 'speakers of the same language' or distant kin or in contemporary usage often simply 'friends') obligations. In desperation Mona turned to prostitution to supplement the family income. Her husband did not know as she 'worked' during the day while he was at his job. The demands of a sex worker and the consequences of her deceit if discovered affected her negatively. She abused alcohol and gambled and little of her income went into the household. Her husband drank and gambled with her and they fought a lot. Mona gave birth two more children and their economic situation became desperate. There was little food and no money for school fees. Then Mona *painum Jisus* (TP: found Jesus or converted to Christianity) and ceased to *pulim man*, consume alcohol and gamble. The family moved to more arable land outside town. They had no running water or sanitation but Mona preferred it because she could grow vegetables for consumption or sale.

Another ex-prostitute said many young women who have not been to school and *no kisim save long rid na rite* (TP: are illiterate) resort to prostitution and infant abandonment, and that the mortality rate of unwanted babies is high. Other women say that PNG men expect subservience from their women whether wives, girlfriends or workmates. While it is socially acceptable for married men to practice infidelity, it is not acceptable for married women who are beaten, killed or jailed for adultery—a criminal offence punishable by imprisonment. Women say men from patriarchal lineages are worse. They beat their wives, are philanderers and often do not support their children. Women in such relationships often resort to prostitution to survive. I was told about a PNG woman, with three young children, whose husband beat her, slept with other women and did not provide for her or the children. To survive, she sold betel nut and cigarettes and dabbled in prostitution. When her husband returned from cavorting they drank and smoked and chewed (betel nut) together, and their children were left to 'run wild and beg for food' from neighbours.

Bomana male prisoners and ex-prisoners say many boys are expelled from home or choose to leave for reasons of deprivation and abuse, sexual, physical or emotional. Many of these angry young men with few formal or informal work opportunities to prove their social and economic legitimacy, are initiated into manhood through alcohol and marijuana abuse and a criminal act such as carjacking and armed robbery. Victims are stabbed, shot or raped even after they relinquish their possessions, and court officials believe there are 'more crimes of violence of an isolated nature'. Beyond such viciousness, criminals are doing what the Government is not; that is, redistributing income to those who are unable to find formal employment (Levantis 1997). But often 'the boundaries are blurred' between legitimate and illegitimate activities, suggesting an exploitation of the uneducated poor by some members of the educated élite (Harris 1998).

Conclusion

The exotic history and high cultures of first-contact Papua New Guinea were crushed under the colonial machine. The over-bureaucratised, underdeveloped and under-resourced bureaucracy at Independence spelt long-term political, economic and social disaster for the country. Crime is now beyond manageable proportions and corruption is endemic. Analysing it and its control within the historical, demographic and socio-economic environments of Papua New Guinea is complex. The impact of a weak and corrupt administration, exploding population, depleted government services, constant political change, and a depressed economy add to its complexity and to the challenge of management. The economy has stagnated, corruption amongst constitutional office holders is rife, the unemployed youth population has exploded, crimes of violence have escalated, more girls and women are selling sex and marijuana and teams of children roam city streets begging for 'coin'. Educated sophisticates aligned with criminal gangs exploit the increasing pool of poor, uneducated youth and well-planned and organised criminal operations redistribute goods and services, protect the élite and drain meagre state resources.

Note

1 This estimate is calculated from person numbers per rural district contained in the 'Preliminary Figures' report of the PNG 2000 Census conducted by the National Statistical Office, Port Moresby.

2
Politics, the economy and law enforcement

The politics of law enforcement

On 1 December 1998, in a full-page newspaper advertisement, Central Province Governor Ted Diro, lamented the 'collapse' of the PNG parliamentary system due to 'under-resourcing' and because committee chairmen had 'become recipients of Prime Ministerial favour losing their independence as guardians of the public purse'. In particular, he referred to the 'evaporation of opposition to the 1999 Budget' after the ultimatum of Prime Minister Bill Skate—no Budget support, no 'access to development funds'—meaning, ministers would not get their 'slush funds' unless they supported the Budget. Diro also referred to the 'almost weekly turnover in ministers and vice ministers' and the lack of accountability and monitoring of public expenditure and ministerial performance due to a weak Onbudsman commission and ineffective Auditor-General, Public Accounts and Public Works Committees (Diro 1998a).

On 30 November 1999, the new Prime Minister, Sir Mekere Morauta, handed down the 2000 Budget. To ensure it was passed within the fragile, corrupt and changeable political environment, he used the strategy of appeasement. He allowed politicians to keep their controversial Rural Development Funds—their 'slush funds'—admitting it would be 'political suicide' not to and realising his decision would bring criticism.

It came quickly. Professor of Law at the University of Papua New Guinea, John Nonggorr, said 'all odds are stacked against a truly accountable system' if the Prime Minister needs to 'cut [unethical] deals' to stay in office and Sir Anthony Siaguru, head of Transparency International in Papua New Guinea, pointed out that prime ministerial bribes undermine the integrity of that office (Nonggorr 1999, Siaguru 2000b). At the Prime Minister's breakfast, the day after the 2000 Budget was handed down, the Managing Director of the PNG branch of the international chartered accountancy firm, Price Waterhouse Cooper, said the PNG Government was plagued by corruption, nepotism, mismanagement and self-interest and there were no easy short-term solutions. At the same time the Chief Ombudsman, Simon Pentanu, suggested a Code of Ethics for politicians and public servants because two weeks before fraud had been alleged against a former Prime Minister. The National Provident Fund, a workers' superannuation fund, had been abused by 'politicians putting their hands in the till…'—contributing to a debt of K60 million—and the Central Bank had been 'raided by the Skate Government' of K1.2 billion (Hiambohn 1999a:1, Sela 1999b:1).

Papua New Guinea politics is fluid and volatile with frequent changes and reconciliations. Over the past five years there have been three prime ministers and three governments and several changes of ministries in each government. The Prime Minister in 2001, Sir Mekere Morauta, held senior posts in the Skate Government including membership of budgetary committees. When he became Prime Minister he appointed no less than 17 Ministers who had held portfolios in the discredited Skate Government, moreover half the NEC (or Cabinet) Members had been Members of that government. No-confidence votes moved in the first six months of each year have brought down successive PNG Governments. Aware of this, Prime Minister Skate and Prime Minister Morauta adjourned Parliament for the first six months of 1999 and 2001 respectively. In adjourning Parliament to July 2001 Sir Mekere said 'neither I nor any other members of the government can afford to have our achievements undone for reasons of political expediency' and 'Papua New Guinea remains a very fragile state—one wrong move and we lose the lot—we lose it forever' (CNN 13 November 2000). The adjournment of Parliament meant that legislation on the political integrity and stability bills designed to stop MPs leaving their party during a parliamentary term and to stop them from crossing the floor to vote against their parties on key issues, was postponed. The 2001 Budget called 'Recovery to Reconstruction' was brought down on 28 November 2000. While constrained by outstanding debts and the demands of MPs, it built on the 2000 Budget that had met its fiscal targets and was designed to consolidate the reconstruction process that, it was hoped, would eventually lead to real gains in social and economic development.

The Morauta Government moved the country from a K446.7 million budget deficit in 1999 to projected deficits in 2000 of K137.1 million and in 2001 of K140.0 million. Arrears totalling K320 million from previous governments were settled and K267.9 million was allocated to further reduce domestic debt. Of the total 2001 appropriation of K3,968.7 million, K1,006.4 million was allocated to pay off and reconstruct debts. While debt reduction was essential for the economic health of Papua New Guinea—saving a huge interest bill of K410 million—it sapped resources away from law enforcement and other priority sectors. Only K2,962.3 million was left to meet all financial commitments to the health, education, law and order, infrastructure and other priority sectors. For their recurrent budgets, these sectors shared an appropriation of only K639.8 million—inadequate to meet the rising costs of basic operational expenses including stationary, equipment and vehicle maintenance, staff transfers, and wages and salaries which had increased by 8 per cent. In stark contrast, MPs maintained K143.5 million for their 'slush' funds—K89 million in Rural Development Funds and K54.5 million in provincial and district support grants—monies which remain largely unaudited and as investment vehicles, leave a lot to be desired. While domestic revenue was projected to increase by 7.5 per cent, aid grants—mainly from Australia—remained unchanged at K550 million. An extra 15.1 per cent was pegged for the Development Budget or Public Investment Program (PIP) to meet the government's commitment towards development projects. A key initiative of the PIP is the Development Charter Program that allocates K109 million to improve the delivery of basic services under commitments entered into by the National Government with provinces under the National Charter on Reconstruction and Development.

The 2001 fiscal program was designed to tighten public spending, improve debt management, increase the size of the PIP and shift expenditure, if only minimally, to high priority sectors. Gross domestic product (GDP) was projected to grow by 3.1 per cent in 2001, by 5.7 per cent in 2002 and by 8 per cent in 2003. More responsible economic and financial management by the government had stabilised the kina at US$0.33 and foreign exchange reserves had trebled to US$279.5 million. With interest rate falls, banks began lowering lending rates and inflation was also reduced by 10 per cent to 12.2 per cent. The Prime Minister said the quarterly increase in inflation of only 0.9 per cent 'shows that the prudent and responsible economic policies of the government are bearing fruit', that performance 'showed that with proper management Papua New Guinea has the capacity to repair the disasters inflicted on the country by the previous government' but that 'much more hard work remained to be done' to address the 'very severe consequences' of the inherited 'economic mess'. On 23 February 2001, a public sector structural reform program, including a corporate and management action plan targeting governance, sustainable macroeconomic activity and public sector performance, was launched. Its estimated cost was K65.8 million (*Post-Courier* 26 February 2001). In early March 2001, the NEC approved proposals to reform and boost morale in the Defence Force and the Defence Department to restore defence capacity and, seven months later, the Prime Minister 'promised a hefty K35 million to rebuild the Defence Force' (Kone 2001:1).

Economic growth projections, however, were based on expected increases in export prices—that did not eventuate in most commodities—and on political stability and the implementation of the Structural Reform Program which promised the injection of a total of US$300 million from the World Bank, International Monetary

Fund (IMF), Australia and Japan. The conditions for such support were improved central bank independence, strengthening supervision of financial institutions, reform of the public sector and privatisation of certain public enterprises. By early November 2001, the only condition met was the restoration of the independence of the Bank of Papua New Guinea with the passing of amendments to the Central Banking Act. None of the other conditions had been met due, the IMF believed to 'limited technical capacity to implement a broad range of agreed measures in many policy areas'. In lieu of the receipt of tranches for that year of US$90 million from the World Bank when certain government institutions were privatised, US$25 million from Japan conditional upon progress in several structural areas, and US$25 million from the Asian Development Bank conditional upon certain administrative improvements in the public sector, the government was expected to resort to domestic borrowing (Waram 2001a:3). Yet public sector reform can be achieved with political will and adequate resource commitments to put in place certain basic legislative and administrative elements to fight the range of ills afflicting government: corruption, *wantok*ism, nepotism, regionalism and political interference. Passing the Integrity of Political Parties and Candidates Act (the political integrity bill) is the first step. The second is to apply it through administrative processes including an effective Parliamentary Accounts Committee, an effective Central Agencies Coordinating Committee, and a strengthened Auditor-General, Ombudsman Commission, Attorney-General and Central Supply and Tenders Board. These very basic elements of public sector reform can be achieved with political will and perseverance, as can the privatisation of public utilities and institutions such as the PNG Banking Corporation and Air Nuigini, and the supervision and regulation by the Central Bank of all financial institutions. In so doing, major benefits would ensue: the freeing up of quasi entrepreneurial public servants to be efficient public administrators; the freeing up of funds to pay outstanding debts and to give greater support to priority sectors like education, health and law and order; a significant reduction in fraud and exploitation of public institutions; and a greater assurance of apprehensions, prosecutions and punishments of wrongdoers in public office.

International investor optimism rested on the achievement of the reforms and on the economic advances in 2000 of a 3.3 per cent increase in GDP, the reduction of inflation and interest rates and stabilisation of the exchange rate (Duncan 2001:13). Yet in 2001, optimism again waned when neither the public sector nor the privatisation reform programs were finalised and the release of annual tranches of foreign loans were stymied. In 2002, cash flow problems will worsen, aggravated by the government's long-standing tendency to overspend (the government overspent by K138.3 million in 2000) and the fact that the Standard and Poor downgraded Papua New Guinea's credit worthiness due to its 'high level of sovereign risk' (Duncan 2001:6). This risk status is measured by past performance and future projections—political instability long recognised as a primary factor and manifesting in policy instability, poor governance, corruption and politicisation of the public sector. Resistance to economic reforms is growing as economic growth prospects weaken, and the standby agreement with the IMF will terminate in September 2002. It is not surprising that Papua New Guinea failed to attract new business investment in 2001—especially to the mining sector at a time when output is in secular decline. The Governor of the Bank of Papua New Guinea revised the 2001 GDP growth rate down from the forecast 3.1 per cent to 0.1 per cent due to the delayed release of the US$20 million World Bank loan. Duncan (2001:5) believes the GDP growth forecast was optimistic and dependent upon Papua New Guinea's ability to reduce its sovereign risks by implementing the public sector reform and privatisation programs. Quite simply, the government has not followed through on its political rhetoric. For example, while the PIP was strengthened by increasing the share of government expenditure allocated to development—and in 2001 it was expected to be 9.7 per cent of the Budget—in reality the PIP falls short when projected revenues fail to eventuate, recurrent funds are spent in an unwise manner or are overspent, and development expenditure is subject to 'grand corruption' for reasons which may include over-tendering in construction projects, poor investments or substantial theft of public funds (Duncan 2001:7–8).

In his annual review of the PNG economy, ANZ's senior regional economist, Bernard Shuttleworth, said 'it is difficult to see any growth at all in 2002 with continued declines in most commodity prices, the kina likely to drift downwards and investors becoming increasingly risk averse'. He remarked that the perception of corruption in Papua New Guinea was a very negative factor in attracting foreign investment as was the failure of the government to conform with the IMF/ World Bank programs, and while the country 'is under better management'—part of the problem is that successive governments have not locked in past low inflation rates. This is especially pertinent in view of the fact that Papua New Guinea, a small resource-based economy, has only a few options: to invest in infrastructure (human and economic) as part of a long-term strategy; attract foreign investment; reduce government spending and wait for commodity prices to improve (Waram 2001a:1–2).

While the success of future Budgets and the attraction of foreign investors is dependent upon the integrity and accountability of political leaders and the stability of the government, simply keeping the governing coalition together, on course and functioning at a minimal level, has been a major feat given the constant threats and infighting—designed to upset the balance of power. Papua New Guinea political parties lack a mass base. This perpetuates the weakness of the PNG State inhibiting consistent governance and law enforcement. Election campaigning is based on traditional redistributive relationships, with leaders providing resources to supporters on the understanding that such favours will be repaid with interest. The long-running first-past-the-post method of electing parliamentary representatives, where up to 40 candidates compete and can achieve office with only 20 per cent of the vote, encourages parochial interests, reinforces political, social and economic fragmentation and defies all efforts to ensure accountability. It is hoped that the preferential voting system, if endorsed by Parliament for the 2007 national elections, will make for more predictable politics and more equitable representation (Taimbari 2001:5). In the meantime, the merging of four political parties to form the People's National Alliance in December 1999 appears to be a move away from independent representation that has characterised PNG politics since independence (Joku 1999b:1).

The Law on Integrity of Political Parties and Candidates shows promise as a regulator of stability and greater accountability in political circles. Under Sections 20 and 21 of the law, a list of political parties must be published in the National Gazette as soon as practical after the date of issue of writ for a National Election. The political party must apply for registration within a certain timeframe and name its office holders who must sign statutory declarations that they are members of that party only. It is hoped that application of the law will reduce the number of independent candidates as well as last minute switches by individuals between parties—behaviour that destabilises coalitions and undermines governance. The political integrity bill is also designed to provide a legal mechanism to increase goods and services to citizens by holding to account, through an Independent Commission Against Corruption, unscrupulous politicians who mismanage government resources, siphon off resources to support political ambitions or cement alliances, and steal from the public purse. There has been only one debate on the bill and a reluctance by Parliament to pass it because, if made retrospective, 'half the Members of Parliament [would end] up in jail' (Ame 2001:4). Resource scarcity has made occupancy of state institutions and alliance with, or support of, office holders an essential way to access goods and services—politics becoming a *bisnis* (TP: business). Elected candidates gain access to resources for personal use or for redistribution to those instrumental in maintaining office who may be the politician's *lain* (TP: extended family or clan group), or individuals and groups allied with politicians in relationships of reciprocity. In view of this, Sir Anthony Siaguru of Transparency International Papua New Guinea believes the political integrity bill is too important not to pass, and has advocated an amnesty for allegedly corrupt politicians to ensure it is passed. However, if the decision is to 'move on' from past gross misdemeanours, the challenge will be to ensure that administrative processes are well resourced to apply the legislation to avoid a further fall in public confidence.

Reciprocity networks between politicians, public servants, criminal gangs and citizens flourish. Networks are perpetuated by ethnicity or other alliances; fear, need and greed block crime control efforts that respond selectively rather than effectively. It is often said, 'it is safer to know a few rascals', than not. Criminal gangs align themselves with less reputable politicians and other prominent persons for the reciprocal benefits of information, protection, goods or sanction. In the late 1970s and early 1980s, there were networks between criminals and 'normal' people. These 'normal' people lived in 'ordinary' suburbs, had formal jobs but made the most of opportunities to explore residential and business break and enter possibilities and to tip off gangs. Their rewards were either material benefits from criminal activity or protection by a gang. Also, some less reputable politicians and other prominent persons either led, or were involved in gangs. As gangs grew in number the operational unit for specific actions became smaller and more specialised, distribution networks expanded and crimes became better targeted (Harris 1998). In December 1999, in Port Moresby, a rascal gang hijacked a helicopter to rob the Bank of Papua New Guinea. Hearsay suggests that a serving politician orchestrated the heist, employing his relatives and their friends to rob the bank. The heist failed and police shot and killed all potential robbers, even those who surrendered. The ringleaders of the attempted robbery have so far not been identified.

My last experience of reciprocity for protection occurred when I lived alone in an old house in Port Moresby in 1997 and 1998. While I had a guard who lived on the property, he had to sleep and go out from time to time. During his absences I was vulnerable to attack. One day a young man, whom I shall call 'Jo' came to my gate and told me his youth group was protecting that area. They had already caught two criminals, and after 'bashing them up to teach them a lesson', handed them over to police. Jo said that if I paid K20 per month 'donation' I would be protected from rape and robbery. He showed me evidence that his youth group came under the umbrella of the Port Moresby Youth Network. He said all group members, including him, had been 'in jail' and were 'hard core criminals' and guarded former Prime Minister Skate. I gladly paid the 'insurance' and was never robbed or raped. Jo collected the money monthly and always issued a receipt. One day he turned up to collect the money in a police vehicle with a carton of beer on the back seat.

A senior public servant told me of a reciprocity relationship he and his family had with 'homeless' youth. He said, 'I look after them and they look after my family and me. I don't ask them what they do at night'. 'Rascal networks' also help to recover stolen cars and computers. For example, representatives of a government agency contacted a juvenile gang and an adult gang to recover two cars stolen in Port Moresby in 1998 and 1999. Deals were done and the vehicles returned. In another incident, computers stolen from a government agency were recovered from the businessman to whom they had been sold, who demanded compensation for their loss. A deal was done and the computers returned. The police were not contacted in any of these cases.

The Sandline Affair and its implications for law enforcement

In April 1997 a constitutional crisis—the Sandline Affair—occurred when the Prime Minister Sir Julius Chan, his Deputy Chris Haiveta and others, were alleged to have conspired with foreign mercenaries to quell by force the seven-year-old rebellion in the North Solomons Province, at a cost of US$36 million. The rebels sought secession from Papua New Guinea and compensation for resources damaged by the Bougainville Copper Mine. The Sandline Affair tested Papua New Guinea's democracy and its morality. Papua New Guinea Defence Force (PNGDF) Commander Jerry Singirok led a revolt against the government's Sandline initiative, demanding that Chan and Haiveta stand down from office. The PNGDF surrounded Parliament House keeping Ministers hostage until a decision was made. Protests were staged for the international media outside Parliament House. It was commonly believed that rascal groups were paid by certain politicians to protest with a view to bringing down the Chan/Haiveta Government. I lived opposite Parliament House at the time of the crisis and walked with a friend amongst protestors to the front gates of the building. Women street vendors selling iceblocks, drinks, eggs and scones lined the road to the gates. We chatted with policemen and PNGDF personnel, hailing 'good afternoons' to other pedestrians. We saw Australian Channel Nine journalists, their cameras mounted on the back of a utility, rehearsing protest groups then doing first and second takes of 'protesting' action. Next morning, Chan and Haiveta stood down, the mercenaries were expelled from the country and two Commissions of Inquiry, the Los and the Andrew Commissions, were established to investigate allegations of corruption associated with the affair. Those implicated were Prime Minister Sir Julius Chan, Deputy Prime Minister Chris Haiveta, Defence Minister Mathias Ijape, State Solicitor Zachary Gelu, Papua New Guinea Banking Corporation Managing Director Rupa Mulina, Bank of Papua New Guinea Governor Koiari Tarafa and Colonial Aikung of the Defence Force. PNGDF Commander Jerry Singirok was himself later found to have received bribes from a British equipment supplier (Nonggorr 1998c).

Expectations were high that justice would be done through the Andrew and Los Commissions. In both instances, the terms of reference were restricted, first by Sir Julius Chan in relation to the Andrew Commission, and later by Bill Skate in relation to the Los Commission. While the Andrew Commission discovered no firm wrongdoing by individuals, it raised serious questions about the conduct of some individuals. Both commissions found that, although Sir Julius had not corruptly benefited from the Sandline contract, he was ultimately responsible as the head of state for the way in which the contract was signed and the monies transmitted. In relation to Chris Haiveta, both commissions found he had received corrupt monies totalling US$500,000 and had perjured himself four times when he lied about it and other related actions. The commissions also found Mr Haiveta responsible for the way the contract was signed and monies of US$18 million transmitted (Nonggorr 1998e, Donigi 1998). Among other findings, the Los Commission found the Defence Minister, Mathias Ijape, had received all or part of a US$500,000 bribe, Jerry Singirok had received about K71,000 from British arms dealer J&S Franklin (banked into a Swiss bank account) and State Solicitor Zachary Gelu had given advice to Chris Haiveta to split up the Sandline contract price monies into lots of K500,000 to execute separate contracts to bring the transactions within the Public Finances (Management) Act. The commission also found that PNGBC Managing Director Rupa Mulina had assisted Haiveta to send payments to Sandline. While both the Andrew and Los Commissions recommended authorities take action that included prosecution of alleged offenders, nothing has been done.

On 14 October 1998, former Prime Minister Bill Skate re-instated Singirok who had been deposed when his bribe was discovered. Skate defended him, stating that some politicians were 'making more than K70,000' (*Post-Courier* 15 October 1998:2, 19 October 1998:3). Though Singirok is now no longer PNGDF head, he has—like the others who were fraudulently implicated—walked away from the affair virtually unpunished. Skate also reconciled with Haiveta at a lavish 'traditional' compensation ceremony in Port Moresby at taxpayers' expense and on 3 June 1999, made him Deputy Prime Minister. In July 1999 Haiveta switched sides and became Minister for Labour and Employment, then Minister for Petroleum and Energy in the Morauta Government.

These events illustrate the overwhelming self-interest of some politicians and the changeability of alliances amongst political leaders—both impeding governance. A full-page advertisement by two politicians in November 1998 also illustrates how leaders, alleged to have defrauded PNG citizens, are excused from prosecution and punishment—action that, if strong and public enough, would deter further misconduct. The naïve advertisement stated 'our actions of March 1997 put an end to ten years of bloody war...a real Melanesian approach'. It implored the police, defence force and public to let the events be 'a lesson to all of us' acknowledging 'we all make mistakes' and suggesting '[we move on] to heal our nation by addressing our many common concerns...' (Parkop and Roywoiwabal 1998:17). The authors failed to face the reality that strongly deterring such gross misconduct by leaders through prosecution and punishment is a core desire of citizens and central to the ability of a nation 'to heal' and 'to move on'. Instead, the law was compromised by political and personal economic gain. While the Ombudsman Commission investigated Singirok under the Leadership Code, Haiveta has not been prosecuted. Nonggorr believes the issues dealt with by the Andrew and Los Commissions and the ones not dealt with, are too important to ignore and that a similar situation will occur again if reforms are not made to the political system to make it more accountable. However Nonggorr, like Siaguru, advocates an amnesty for allegedly corrupt politicians who remain Members of Parliament to ensure the political integrity bill is passed. Donigi believes, however, that outstanding issues must be dealt with, because the integrity of the law was severely damaged when the formal process of vetting and considering contracts by the NEC was not followed, the process of arbitration simply protecting Chan, Haiveta and their partners (Nonggorr 1998e, 1998g, 1998h; Donigi 1998).

The public, politics and law enforcement

Well-publicised political corruption like that associated with the Sandline Affair and the subsequent inaction by the government to prosecute alleged offenders has enhanced the value of cheating. Any social system with rules of conduct is at risk of individuals cheating when they see the advantages of cheating outweigh the burden of sanctions (see for example Diamond 1991). The PNG public has seen how corrupt and unaccountable their politicians are, how politicised the public service is, and how ineffectual law enforcement agencies are in prosecuting offenders. They see allegedly fraudulent politicians and public servants remaining in positions of trust and power while 'small criminals' and political scapegoats languish in jails. While the Morauta Government has worked hard to improve credibility and accountability, disillusionment runs deep and law and order agencies remain inefficient and under-resourced—the impact of 25 years of ineffectualness is hard to turn around. More than one three-year term of strong, decisive leadership is required to ensure reforms are implemented, but prime ministerial terms tend to be short. From time to time allegedly fraudulent leaders are apprehended and prosecutions begun. It is certainly encouraging that one MP appeared before the Leadership Tribunal for recommending his brother for a senior public service post, and another was arrested for allegedly stealing half a million kina. Yet worthwhile prosecutions and punishments must follow. In committing Opposition Leader and former Prime Minister Bill Skate for trial at the National Court on 22 October 2001, Deputy Chief Magistrate, John Namapo, said there was 'a lot the [police] prosecution has to fix' to succeed in the case. Two counts of misappropriating over K300,000 having been alleged against Mr Skate (*Post-Courier* 23 October 2001:2). It follows the discharge of a K27,600 insurance fraud case against Mr Skate on 5 March 2001 by National Court Judge, Les Gavara-Nanu, due to insufficient evidence (*Post-Courier* 28 February, 2–4 March, 6 March 2001). The allegations were that Skate conspired with others in 1990 to burn his vehicle to claim insurance. On 9 March 2001, Skate appeared before the committal court charged with perverting the course of justice—the matter related to the fraud case discharged. It was alleged that Skate influenced key witnesses to change their stories resulting in the discharge (*The National* 13 March 2001).

Many say the court system is corrupt—'insufficient evidence' or inadequate prosecutions are common—and all too often PNG laws are made a mockery of by those with influence and money. Criminals, jailed for crimes they commit, express anger regarding the lack of prosecution, or inadequate prosecution of politicians and other leaders alleged to have committed criminal offences. They demand greater equity in the justice system and until this occurs, resist 'rehabilitation' efforts that are, in any case, haphazard. In February 1998, the newly-elected Minister for the PNGCS, Peter Arul, visited Bomana prison in the National Capital District. Over 500 male prisoners were assembled on a small hill overlooking the dais, from which the Minister harangued the crowd. Mr Arul reiterated the words of previous Ministers, promising better working conditions for correctional service staff, more recognition of their good work, and better housing. He then walked over to the prisoners and espoused the values of rehabilitation, hard work, being model prisoners, becoming good citizens. A young prisoner, whom I shall call 'Lewis,' paced the prisoners' hill, and speaking in Tok Pisin challenged Arul.

> You talk of rehabilitation, you tell us to change our ways, to become good citizens. But politicians who steal millions of kina are not prosecuted. Are they good citizens? We small criminals are arrested for small things. We are bashed by the

> police and forced to live like animals in overcrowded jails where toilets overflow into our kitchen. We have no good food and no greens. We get sick with malaria, scurvy and dysentery and do not have proper health care. We escape and are bashed and some of us are killed. When we are released, you expect us to change, to become 'good citizens'. How can we do this if we have not learned from our leaders how to be good citizens? Why should we change our ways if you leaders do not change yours? You can read and write, you have been to school, you have a good job. Many of us come from settlements, have no families and nowhere to go when we are released. Until you politicians and public servants change, do not expect us to!

In March 2001, at the end of a three-day church-run leadership course, Bomana prisoners challenged leaders to 'live by example', 'have vision', and work in unity. They appealed for more training opportunities (*Post-Courier* 9–11 March 2001). On 26 September 2001, the *Post-Courier* reported the escape of 62 inmates, mainly remand prisoners, due to court delays, overcrowding, poor food, and boredom. Ten days earlier, 18 prisoners had escaped from regional jails, one shot dead on recapture. Citizens protest cronyism and corrupt practice by politicians and public servants in letters to the media: 'Stop the cronyism…' (*The National* 24 November 1999:15); 'Pros ripping off Papua New Guinea…' (*Post-Courier* 26 November 1999:3); 'Dangers of personality politics' (*The National* 1 December 1999:15); 'What does accountability mean' (*The National* 8 December 1999:15). Prisoners question the quality of police investigations into the bashings of escapees with 'iron bars, timber, batons and full beer bottles', and when prisoner witnesses are not interviewed (*Post-Courier* 29 November 1999:2, 3 December 1999:5). The free press stirs public sentiment against cronyism and corruption with numerous and frequent media reports of aberrant leaders. On 13 March 2001, *The National* reported Police Commissioner John Wakon, as saying 'there are two sets of laws': the big and rich people find protection in the justice system while the small people go to jail. He was referring to the alleged payment of K40,000 to an MP from the Foe landowners trust account. The trust account had been established for future generations of landowners of the Kutubu oil fields. Before police could arrest culprits, landowner leaders took out a restraining order against the police to prevent arrests.

When the impotency of law enforcing agencies in prosecuting corrupt leaders is revealed and citizens demand action, the PNG State does one of two things. Either the law enforcers become brutal in their efforts to prove they can catch, prosecute and punish offenders or they do nothing—there is no middle way. The former approach manifests in states of emergency, curfews, raids, frequently publicised arrests and police and prison warder brutality. Courts 'make example' of offenders who commit more prevalent crime like car thefts, break and enter, and rape. The latter approach draws suspicion and hearsay that political parties, or political personalities, influence criminal justice agency officers by virtue of alliance or lineage, creating conflicts of interest between state laws and political alliances. Either approach diverts public attention from demanding firm and consistent action to address corrupt leadership issues. The self-interest of individuals and groups results in the sanctioning of bribes and the harbouring and protecting of criminals. Commitment to the public good is overridden because 'often we insist on our own little interests without having regard to the interests of the nation' (Nonggorr 1998b:17). At the AusAID PNG Economic Update in Port Moresby on 16 November 1999, a senior employee of a government agency said she would not report a criminal member of her family to the police because 'they are my family'.

Nonggorr offers insight regarding why bribery and corruption is reinforced in Papua New Guinea communities and provides an understanding regarding how politicians can so easily bribe their way into Parliament and accept bribes during their terms of office. The example is given of the preference of his clan to vote for a poorly educated political candidate known to be corrupt. Nonggorr favoured a 'sensible, responsible and honest' overseas tertiary-educated candidate. Nonggorr's father told him there were two reasons for the clan's decision. First, the preferred candidate was a clan member, and second, he paid for votes. The group believed the money they were paid would give them something more than they already had, reasoning they had not received government services for the past five years and assuming they would not get any for the next five (Nonggorr 1998f). *Post-Courier* reader, Laka Philip wrote of his experience of the politicisation of a community during a visit to remote Angagoi in the Kerowagi district of Simbu Province. The incident related to the by-election of the Governor's seat of Simbu. Supporters of one candidate had blocked the road and told other clans to vote for their candidate, 'or else you won't use the road'. Then they took advantage of a landslide blocking a road, telling other clans that, as they would be unable to reach the polling booths to vote, their names would be used instead to vote for the aggressors' candidate (Philip 1999:10). Non-provision of rural communities with adequate goods and services prompted both incidents. In his *Post-Courier* article 'Roads to Ruin', Hunt revealed that 80–90 per cent of the PNG highlands population has no education, the rates of illiteracy range from 70–76 per cent in two highlands provinces, maternal death rates at childbirth are higher than other PNG regions and there is very poor access to drinking water. He blames, in part, the state of the roads for these dire conditions, and in turn, blames those politicians who have rorted millions of kina appropriated for road maintenance over the past decade—actual disbursements for road maintenance being only 75 per cent of allocations (2001:11). The enforced isolation of such communities due to the poor state of many rural roads has resulted in a terrible depletion of essential services: few teachers, few schools, few books, few health workers, few health clinics, few medicines, few extension services, and little or no utilities maintenance. It has also resulted in terrible social and economic limitations: the people cannot get their produce to market, their children to school, their families to health clinics (if they are operating) and cannot re-provision. Such communities are condemned to poverty and ignorance until such time as political capacity is maximised through the introduction and application of the political integrity bill and other laws to enforce systems of accountability—thereby freeing up resources currently unattainable. Until then, community politicisation will continue.

The economy and law enforcement

Crime, corruption and poor management continue to cripple the PNG economy, blocking economic development and stifling incentive. Criminal attacks on people and businesses continue to deter foreign investors and local entrepreneurs, and to restrict access to scarce capital. Three severe economic downturns over the past six years aggravated by volcanic eruptions, cyclones, tidal waves and droughts—which together killed over 3,000 people, displaced communities and crippled agriculture—have further stymied attempts to get goods and services to citizens in legitimate ways. The core of Papua New Guinea's problems relates to governance that in turn influences resource availability. It relates to the lack of fiscal policy that maintains a framework of open and accountable institutions and procedures, and has resulted in 'public revenue [being] placed at the whims of unscrupulous behaviour' (Harden 1999:iii).

Papua New Guinea is the richest country in the Pacific. It has large gold and copper deposits, substantial oil and natural gas reserves, plentiful arable land for agriculture, an abundant supply of fresh water, large commercial forests and extensive oceanic fish stocks. The economy relies heavily on exports of minerals, timber, and tree crops such as coffee, cocoa and copra. Coffee remains the most important export crop although palm oil has grown rapidly in recent years. Log exports have also grown substantially from the early 1990s, however the industry has been plagued by corruption and mismanagement and there appears to be little commitment to industry reform attempts. In 2001, apart from slight increases in cocoa and logs, commodity export prices declined due to decreases in world prices. In the mining and oil sector—Papua New Guinea's single most important source of revenue—there was no new investment in exploration, investors deterred by the country's political instability and enormous compensation claims for polluted rivers and ocean beds. With the closure of the Ok Tedi, Porgera and Tolukuma mines over the next decade, mineral royalties at the disposal of government will slow to a trickle (Gomez 2001)—with profound implications for the Budget. At the same time the high costs of living, poor infrastructure, the inefficient and costly utilities—telecommunications, electricity and water—and the high cost of crime prevention deters both current and potential investors in Papua New Guinea. A survey of business costs by Duncan and Lawson (1997) discovered that 63 per cent of businesses considered security to be the most serious problem inhibiting daily operations and expansion.

In 1997, GDP declined by 4.6 per cent and economic shocks combined with an inadequate fiscal response placed Papua New Guinea's macroeconomic management under severe pressure. Since then a depreciated currency, decline in external reserves and high interest rates have resulted in very high costs of living and contractions in formal employment and formal job creation. A 1996–97 World Bank household survey in Papua New Guinea showed that 93 per cent of poor people lived in rural areas with minimal access to health, education and other government services—access that will decline further with an exploding population and equivalent declines in real GDP per capita. As a result, small-scale agriculture and handicraft production for cash income is limited (Harden 1999:ii)—demonstrated in the fact that between 1980 and 1995, Papua New Guinea had only 1.1 per cent per capita economic growth. In 1998 Papua New Guinea's per capita income was US$890—high compared with lower income countries in Asia and the Pacific—but key social and economic indicators were unsatisfactory and stagnant, UN Development Programme ranking Papua New Guinea 129 out of 174 countries on its human development index in that year. In 2000, the situation was worse—Papua New Guinea ranked 133 out of 174 countries—more than 37 per cent of its citizens having minimal access to health, education, water and sanitation.

Despite Papua New Guinea's resource richness, only a small portion of the country's population is benefiting. Barbara Lepani believes that small portion is the indigenous élite in administrative centres. It is they she says, who account for much of the total consumption of essential goods and services (1993:76). This assertion may explain why there is a marked difference in living standards between rural and urban areas and between provinces (Harden 1999:1). In September 1998, the then Rural Development Minister, Jimson Sauk, said a typical PNG village comprises unemployed youth and 'pushed out' public servants. These people make up 70 per cent of Papua New Guinea's population and have nothing to do but play snooker, drink beer and smoke marijuana. Parliamentary Speaker in 2001, Bernard Narakobi, when launching the Foundation for Rural Development Inc. Papua New Guinea, a rural development organisation, said it would take another 1,000 years to develop life in rural villages to a better standard. The UN Population Fund believes a quicker answer is infrastructure support (Palme 1998, *The National* 9 July 1998:16). The Rural Development Program, constituting 16 per cent of the 2000 Budget, was initiated to provide more resources to communities. Instead, it has been the focus of allegations of corruption by the receiving politicians. The K143.5 million Rural Development Program allocation is divided amongst districts and provinces. Each district receives K1.25 million for its District Development Program, and each province receives K250,000 for its Provincial Development Program. Development plans are drawn up and submitted to the Office of National Planning before funds are released to district and provincial planning and Budget priorities committees—chaired by sitting MPs—who administer the money. Another K27.25 million is a discretionary fund or 'slush fund', called the Rural Action Program, from which each district Member and Provincial Governor receives K250,000. While some provincial governments and politicians keep statistics on how monies are spent, others do not, and expenditure has not been audited. To rectify this, the National Research Institute recommended to the Office of National Planning the production of a supplementary paper to the main Budget papers, publishing Rural Development Program appropriations and expenditure (Hunt 1999c). Also contributing to a failure of fiscal management are the politicisation of Budget management (resulting in uneven distribution of resources), discontinuity of policy development, the concentration on symptoms not causes in public sector reform programs, and the advocacy of cosmetic, rather than real solutions.[1] The reality is that unscrupulous leaders in successive governments have abused the trust of constituents—'gutting' the PNG economy and sending it almost bankrupt by mismanagement and corrupt practice. To turn around the immediate financial crisis, a financial package of US$300 million (K810 million) as part of the IMF and World Bank Structural Reform Program, was secured along with an aid advance from the Australian Government (*The National* 10 November 1999:1). Most of the K810 million, however, was used to pay off debts and prop up an inefficient public service.

Policitians, academics and unionists advocate various measures to restore the economy. These include fiscal discipline, reducing the public service and providing incentives for private sector expansion. (Paska 1999, Hunt 1999b, Barter 1998, AusAID 1999, Manning 1999b). Yet over-spending to alleviate poverty will lead to more inflation and a further fall in the value of the kina, and if external funding dries up because the government has not met its public sector reform commitment, 'expenditure restraint would need to be intensified' (Waram 2001a:3). Papua New Guinea citizens want the government to balance its books rather than go into deficit. Kept informed of the government's economic strategy, most citizens are prepared to make sacrifices induced by fiscal discipline if, in the long term, those sacrifices contribute to a greater share of goods and services. In the meantime, there is enormous discontent and little support for the government's economic reform program. Goods and services secured by previous governments beyond the State's financial capacity, have set the country on an economic downspin with debt repayments in 2000 soaking up K791 million, 38 per cent of Papua New Guinea's recurrent expenditure—further reducing financial flexibility and investment in development projects. In 2001 it was proposed to pay K268.9 million of domestic debt using international concessional loans (US$140 million) and proceeds from privatisation (K178 million) (Duncan 2001:3). Neither funding eventuated as already discussed, and cash flow repercussions—in the form of greatly reduced financial appropriations to government agencies in real terms—will be felt in 2002.

In relation to law enforcement, while the RPNGC received an increased allocation from K90 million to K115.6 million in 1999, in real terms, the value of allocations to the RPNGC and the PNGCS was less than in 1997 and 1998 (Hunt 1999c). The government has not contributed to counterpart funding for some years and is not likely to in the foreseeable future. As a result, AusAID-funded institutional strengthening projects in the RPNGC, A-GD and PNGCS continue to prop up operational expenditure by providing certain materials and other support to meet AusAID contractual deadlines. This financial dependency cannot stimulate sustained development, and unless the government allocates adequate and consistent resources to the criminal justice sector before and after the life of aid projects, agency effectiveness will be quashed. In the first three years of the Correctional Service Development Project, 1996–99, little 'institutional strengthening' occurred. There was minimal overall improvement in staff living and working conditions, and in May 2000, a senior correctional officer said, 'nothing has changed' and 'morale is very low'. In August 2001, there was optimism that some institutional strengthening was occurring, and that the aid project may be 'sustainable'. There was also optimism that when the government's economic and structural reform agendas are implemented, there would be greater agency commitment and increased resource support. However running costs remain higher than budget allocations, prisons remain overcrowded—some even closing from time to time due to poor sanitation—management and staff accountability and productivity remain low, and successive government ministers and departmental heads continue to make promises they cannot keep during their short terms in office. Despite numerous requests by prison management to courts and the parole board to accelerate community based orders, in May 2000, Buimo jail in Lae had 200 remandees in a 30-person capacity holding cell and 300 convicted prisoners in a 70-capacity holding facility. In February 2001, the 'prisons boss' was reported as 'angry' as 72 prisoners had escaped over the previous 12 months and a large amount of money had been misappropriated, allegedly by correctional staff (*Post-Courier* 16–18 February 2001). The prison boss expressed similar anger when 47 remand prisoners escaped from Bomana prison on 25 September 2001, suggesting that such prisoners, who make up 75 per cent of the prison population and cost K2.5 million 'to feed and keep', should be held elsewhere (*Post-Courier* 26 September 2001, 1 October 2001). There was glimmer of hope in July 2001 when Justice Minister, Puri Ruing, told the media that 46 inmates considered 'no threat to society' had been screened for release on licence. Expectations were that families of released prisoners, and the community in general, would be responsible for the prisoners' reintegration and rehabilitation, and would report breaches of conditions to supervising community correctional officers—all unrecompensed and with minimal support from government.

The most basic service a State can provide its citizens is security. If the State fails, or becomes a threat to security itself, it cannot exercise authority or expect loyalty in return (Dinnen 1999). With a view to providing better security, it has been suggested that verifiable performance indicators by sector should accompany budget reform—to measure financial, physical, and social performance—and be readily usable by the National Planning Office. For the law and order sector, verifiable performance indicators could be the number of police houses built, the number of trained police deployed by location, and include crime and apprehension rates (Hunt 1999b). State legitimacy is performance-based, because the State competes with hundreds of local societies to win people's support. In relation to law enforcement, this realisation is crucial, because without legitimacy, law and order agencies are ineffectual. Instead, public perceptions of inaction, or inappropriate action, by law enforcers may prompt 'local solutions' which are not state sanctioned. For example, tribal fighting flared over three weeks amongst five clans in November 1999, in Laiagam in Enga Province. The violence resulted in two deaths and the destruction of Laiagam High School (*The National* 25 November 1999:1–3). In the same month in Central Province, a PNG woman I know and her children were attacked in their home by her late husband's relatives with 'new bush knives ready to kill us, smashing windows, tearing flywire and clothing, stealing our things and killing our dogs'. On 5 October 2001, the *Post-Courier* reported that two village court officials on their way to Wabag police station to sort out a tribal fight between the Titi and Mangen clans were ambushed, shot dead, then 'chopped to pieces'.

While performance indicators, political and structural reform, a clear Budget process and delayed consumption may have long-term practical benefits and improve the credibility of law enforcing agencies, all efforts will fail if not initiated within a transparent, accountable framework that emphasises and monitors audit and management commitment at all levels of government, and consistently punishes those who defraud the public. The Morauta Government put urgent emphasis on reforms to meet these needs. The current reality is, however, that some greedy politicians and senior public servants do not turn rhetoric into due process, do deals for personal gain, and steal public monies from PNG taxpayers—knowing their behaviour will rarely be audited and that prosecutions will even more rarely follow. To counter these audit and prosecution deficiencies, infrastructure support must include the development of criminal justice agencies to protect citizens and visitors who are frequently robbed, raped, mugged or killed while waiting on roadsides to sell produce, travelling in private and public motor vehicles, or attempting to see the sights or enjoy a day out with family and friends. Such cowardly crimes reach the international media from time to time and are effective in deterring business investment and tourism. They include the shooting death of a woman on her way to Lae in a PMV to do her Christmas shopping, an attack on eight nuns from Nazareth mission outside Port Moresby—one of whom was 'bashed in the head' and the vehicle stolen (*The National* 7 December 1999:5, *Post-Courier* 10 July 2001)—the attack in 1999 on British volunteers travelling in the highlands when female volunteers were raped, the attack in early 2001 on a group of expatriate and national bushwalkers outside Port Moresby who were bashed and their possessions stolen, the shooting and stabbing deaths and muggings of nationals and expatriates during car hijackings, home invasions and armed robberies, the destruction of project equipment, the theft of motor vehicles, and the numerous attacks on and killings of women and children. Meanwhile, in the national capital, street beggars are increasing—young, old and crippled. Skinny children scavenge for used drink cans to sell, and a crippled young man sits on Saturdays outside a store begging, a small box containing a few coins in front of his twisted limbs. In the town centre, a gang of young boys in dirty, ragged clothes, the oldest not more than ten, work together pick-pocketing or begging for 'coin'. Older boys lead and organise the younger ones, who hold out one upturned hand to passers by, and with the other, point grimy fingers at their mouth, 'Coin?' they ask. '*Mi hangri*' (TP: I'm hungry).

Conclusion

The PNG Constitution emphasises equality and participation for integral human development. It also specifies respect for the rights and freedoms of others and the value of cooperation in the interests of interdependence and solidarity. Yet when politicians allegedly 'put their hands in the till' of a workers' superannuation fund, when former Prime Ministers and their deputies collude with mercenaries, when the Prime Minister decides it would be 'political suicide' not to give politicians several million kina of taxpayers' money to spend as they wish, when politicians buy votes and political factions in government departments use violence to oppose decisions, the political and economic frameworks in which they operate are indeed very weak.

Constant power plays between government ministers resulting in shifts within coalitions that lack a mass base have perpetuated political instability, reinforced the value of nepotism, cronyism and corruption, and restricted public access to goods and services through legitimate channels. The integrity law may reduce such disruptive power plays and allow the same government to govern for its full term of office. In the meantime, less reputable MPs and others exploit criminal gangs, creating flourishing reciprocity networks that provide protection and material benefits or a means of retribution that ignores or manipulates government process to reinforce allegiances. In this environment the control of crime is selective rather than effective and reactionary rather than planned. The effect on the national economy is downward while poverty, disillusionment and crime are perpetuated.

The Sandline crisis offered the PNG State the opportunity to prosecute offenders and send a clear message to potential perpetrators that fraudulent behaviour will not be tolerated. However, respective governments have chosen not to act, choosing instead to compromise the law for political gain and in the interests of 'getting on with the more important issues of governance'. Government inaction in the aftermath simply reinforces the value of cheating, highlights gross inequalities, encourages small criminals to mirror the aberrant behaviour of some leaders, prolongs political instability and widespread corruption, 'guts' the economy further, destroys investor confidence and depletes real financial allocations to under-resourced justice agencies.

Expectations are high, nationally and internationally, about what Papua New Guinea can achieve as a nation-state. More business investors will invest in Papua New Guinea and more tourists will visit Papua New Guinea when they feel safe, when there is reliable infrastructure, and when there is a more stable government. But when there is a high probability of being mugged, robbed or raped, a high probability of not being able to meet market demands, and a high probability of having to pay bribes to corrupt officials to keep the telephones and electricity on, many investors and visitors prefer not to waste their time and risk their money in an environment where their property and personal rights are not protected.

Note

1 Authorless and untitled article in *The Independent* reporting on comments made by visiting Australian National University academic, Brian Brogan (*The Independent* 29 May 1998:19).

3
Crime and criminal justice agencies

Papua New Guinea is perceived as a violent and dangerous place. The PNG media reports brutal and violent crime, especially armed robbery and rape almost daily, and property crime is blatant and endemic in urban centres like Port Moresby and Lae (Levantis and Chand 1997). For example on a Saturday morning in June 2000 two criminals stole my partner's car as he put air in a front tyre at a local petrol station. He was punched in the face as he wrestled for the keys. I know at least five other people, nationals and expatriates, to whom this has occurred—two were knifed and badly injured. An international victimisation survey conducted by the United Nations Interregional Crime and Justice Research Institute, which compared law and order in PNG urban centres with 12 other surveyed cities in Latin America, Africa and Asia—including Johannesburg, Rio de Janeiro, Dar Es Salaam and Kampala—found that, across most crime categories, PNG urban centres fared worst, and had the highest incidence of sexual assault (Levantis 2000:132, Zvekic and Alvazzi 1995, Zvekic and Weatherburn 1995). While most PNG citizens do not know the extent of crime in their country compared with other countries, they nevertheless express concern regarding the negative impact of crime on themselves as victims, and on their country's political, social and economic growth. They simply do not feel safe and do not believe their property is safe. These feelings of danger immobilise them and stop many worthwhile social and economic activities from occurring. A common statement is 'I love my country...but the crime!'. Foreign residents commonly say 'It's a great place except for the crime'. Crime and violence costs Papua New Guinea an estimated 300–400 million kina per year in lost business and tourism opportunities and it is believed to be the single biggest deterrent to business and investment (Duncan and Lawson 1997).

In the late 1990s, reports of serious crime in Papua New Guinea averaged about 11,500 a year—fully 65 per cent higher than 10 years before. Most crime is reported in urban areas, particularly the NCD which accounts for 50 per cent of reported crime—this higher rate due, the police believe, to accessibility to police and police stations to make reports. The most prevalent serious crime in 1998 was robbery, followed by break and enter, car theft, serious sexual, then drug related offences (see Table 1). Rape and pack rape is common, many victims abducted from roadsides (*The National* 15 March 1999:8, Clifford, Morauta and Stuart 1984a). Reports of domestic violence are increasing and there is a history of police failure to act on reports. For example, the police response to an attack by a man on his wife, who was killed, was, 'It's a family matter and should be dealt with by the family' (*Post-Courier* 23 February 2000:2).

Estimates of reported crime vary from 10–30 per cent to not more than 50 per cent (Levantis 1997) and crime cases cleared by police—usually a result of the crime being solved—is less than 50 per cent of those reported. Unknown is the full extent of crime, accurate community perceptions of crime or of criminal justice problems, why only some crime is reported, and the different ways in which communities resolve conflicts (Zvekic and Weatherburn 1993). Nevertheless, anecdotal evidence suggests that the low clearance rate of reported crime and estimates of crime, not reported, probably have several causes. These include the ability to report crime, a lack of confidence in the police, deficiencies in police reporting and fear

Table 1 Reported number of serious crimes in Papua New Guinea, 1980–98

Crime	1980	1986	1990	1996	1997	1998	Percentage increase/ decrease (1986–98)[z]
Murder	127	285	289	499	459	502	43.2
Serious sexual offences [x]	285	774	1032	1208	1392	1513	48.8
Grievous bodily harm	..	558	705	855	897	996	43.9
Robbery	530	771	1423	2021	2815	2215	65.1
Breaking and entering	2438	3594	3539	2597	2433	2100	-41.5
Car theft	..	142	530	688	1525	1739	91.8
Stealing	..	..	..	510	615	743	31.3 (96/98)
Fraud and misappropriation	..	..	..	228	190	236	3.3 (96/98)
Escape from prison	..	..	..	144	138	235	38.7
Drug related	..	87	271	1397	763	1012	91.4
Firearm offences	..	53	83	336	382	374	85.8
Escape from police	..	..	..	309	276	404	23.5
Total	6199	6960	8720	10792	11888	12069	48.6
Clearance rate (%)[y]	..	53.9	34.9	47.8	39.1	49.4	-4.5

Notes: [x] It is believed that only 30–40 per cent of sexual crimes are reported and, of those reported, a portion are classified as grievous bodily harm.

[y] Clearance rate reflects the percentage of cases that are closed or cleared, usually as a result of being solved.

[z] Percentage increase/decrease column has been added to reveal overall increases in crime.

Source: Royal Papua New Guinea Constabulary.

and obligations in the networks that surround offenders. Anecdotal evidence also suggests that complainants often prefer to resolve matters independently. I have already mentioned the case of the rape of a girl that was 'resolved' through the village court. Her family did not want to report the crime to police because of 'family shame', preferring to take compensation from the perpetrator's family, with a village court magistrate acting as mediator. Serious assaults, armed robbery and break and enter are often not reported to the police because 'they do nothing'. Instead, they are resolved by either mutually agreed compensation or by payback muggings, killings or property damage—again these are often not reported to police for fear of further retribution by individuals or criminal gangs. Police sources say five bosses control crime in Papua New Guinea. The crime bosses lead 150–200 specialised career criminals and some 50,000 young and uneducated operatives. The network allegedly has links to political and government circles in the form of reciprocity arrangements providing mutual benefits like information, protection and material advantage. For example in February 2000, it was reported that politicians and prominent leaders were allegedly involved in crime in the Southern Highlands Province and interfered with the National Government's initiative to combat crime there (*Post-Courier* 4 February 2000:3).

Rascals come from a wide range of socio-economic backgrounds, graduating to serious crime from a range of minor criminal activities. They may at the same time be in legitimate employment. Social relations of criminal gangs are typical of pre-capitalist societies regarding acquisition of gift debtors—the modern gangs integrate pre-capitalist social relations into a cash economy (Goddard 1995, Harris 1998, Dinnen 1998). In Papua New Guinea, the expectation of giving and taking gifts is central to social relationships within the modern cash economy. A gift may be in cash, kind or a service, the value of it measured in terms of the perceived value of the gift as well as the perceived wealth of the giver. Distribution is governed by the perceived status of giver and receiver within a group hierarchy. It is common for lower-income persons to adopt patrons who will protect them and provide financial and other assistance from time to time. Generally, the patron is expected to take a negotiated action, or give a negotiated gift in return for loyalty or a service. I have been in relationships with low-income earners from whom I received services like protection, gardening, housework and language tuition. As well as paying in cash, I gave food and other gifts in kind that would generate income, for example school fees or tools. Some influential people act as patrons to 'youth groups' with low or no education and few job options, whose members may continue to participate in illicit activity. The arrangement is that the youths protect the patron's family, property and business in return for money, food and shelter—or protection from prosecution.

Some criminals like to believe they commit 'Robin Hood' crimes—taking from the rich and giving to the poor, or to their families—but this does not account for the enormous number of reported rape and other sexual attacks on women and children and the increase in reported vicious crime. While larger material returns from crime are commonly used to mobilise support for political ambitions (Goddard 1992b), more often the poor and vulnerable are mugged, robbed, raped and killed for their meagre wages and are easy targets in highway attacks—rarely reporting incidences for fear of retribution. For example in 1999, an elderly man I know was robbed twice at knifepoint of his weekly earnings of K50 as he walked home from Koki market in Port Moresby, a distance of one kilometre. A woman I know was threatened at knifepoint by a gang of adolescents as she walked along a major thoroughfare, and another was stabbed in the stomach and robbed while travelling home in a PMV. The woman threatened at knifepoint believes it is safer to walk with a child to deter rapists. She said women who are raped in her settlement do not report the crime for fear of beatings by their husbands or families because of the shame of the rape. There is also a belief that the police 'will do nothing' or perhaps rape the victim as well. I too have been harassed in the town centre by men seeking sexual favours and have been followed to my car and to my place of work.

Alphonse Jimu, a Port Moresby Police Station Commander in 1989, told the 81st International Seminar on Advancement of the Integration of the Criminal Justice Administration in Tokyo, that socially dislocated PNG children who commit crime are usually grade six dropouts who 'look for something to keep them busy and when they are hungry steal a loaf of bread or a biscuit', then steal 'more and more and...eventually end up in prison' (Jimu 1989:250). All but one of the juvenile prisoners at Bomana prison in April 1997 had never been to school. As well as crimes perpetrated by desperate, disillusioned youth, crimes of violence between ethnic groups are common and usually committed in vengeance. Twenty-one thousand crimes of ethnic violence were reported between 1986 and 1990 in Papua New Guinea—National Court files documenting much ethnic-based crime. For example, in the Port Moresby suburb of Morata in 1998 an Eastern Highlands couple was killed and mutilated in retaliation for an assault by an Eastern Highlands man on members of the perpetrating ethnic group. In another incident a young man from Bereina in Central Province attempted to kill an Engan man for a serious assault on his father.

Crime trends

Criminal justice statistics in Papua New Guinea are notoriously unreliable. They either suffer from non-reporting or non-recording, and in addition may be inaccurate. This makes it difficult to assess levels of crime, prosecutions, incarceration and community-based supervision of offenders. Shortcomings in the capacity of agencies are apparent in detection, investigation, the penetration of criminal justice agencies into communities and reporting (Zvekic and Weatherburn 1993).

The police

Table 1 shows available statistics on reported serious crime in Papua New Guinea between 1980 and 1998. The table indicates that in the 12 years from 1986 to 1998 reported crime doubled to almost 12,069 incidents. Robbery, breaking and entering, car theft and serious sexual offences were the most prevalent crimes recorded in 1998 and from 1986 drug related crimes and car thefts rose by 91 per cent, firearm offences by almost 85 per cent, robbery by 65 per cent, murder, sexual offences and grievous bodily harm by more than 43 per cent and stealing by 31 per cent. Notwithstanding their unreliability, the statistics appear to confirm the opinion of police and national court spokespersons that crime is becoming more vicious and better-planned and orchestrated, and robbery and car theft more frequent. Marijuana is commonly consumed before criminal operations and firearms are used during operations. Papua New Guinea marijuana commonly called 'New Guinea gold' is very strong and can cause early psychosis in frequent users and aggressive mood swings when consumed with alcohol. It is sought widely internationally and has become a lucrative illicit cash crop—the proceeds of which some say, is used to buy guns.

Table 1 also shows a 41 per cent decrease in break and enter and only a 3.3 per cent increase in fraudulent offences. The decrease in break and enter could be for several reasons. For example, fewer crimes are reported to police because of the perception 'they [the police] don't do anything', houses are better secured, or there is a significant change in crime patterns, in that crimes are better targeted, and there are increased opportunities to prey on more vulnerable persons whose homes are without bars, razor wire and security guards. The minor increase in reported fraud is at odds with public opinion on the frequency of such offences indicating perhaps inadequate police fraud investigative skills, inaction by persons in positions of power for fear of violent retribution, or fear of loss of political allegiance. Community complacency too often condones such acts as an essential part of 'traditional' socio-economic relations to obtain resources. The rise in prison escapes of almost 39 per cent and the rise in escapes from police of over 23 per cent, appear to confirm media and other reports that prisons, police and courts are over-stretched and unable to cope.

The poor and vulnerable do not fare well in Papua New Guinea. They are either victimised by criminals or incarcerated themselves for petty crime, while prosecutions of alleged fraud by persons in positions of trust rarely eventuate. Brother Graeme Frawley, the National Director of Caritas, a Catholic run organisation that lobbies for community justice and provides training and welfare services in Papua New Guinea and elsewhere, believes Papua New Guinea's

Table 2 **Reported/recorded offences and arrests for serious crime in Papua New Guinea,** January to May 1997 and 1998

	January–May 1997			January–May 1998		
	Offences	Arrests	%	Offences	Arrests	%
Murder	182	180	98.9	193	179	92.7
Serious sexual offences	417	239	57.3	688	225	32.7
Grievous bodily harm/wounding	222	118	53.1	424	184	43.3
Robbery	997	537	53.8	991	382	38.5
Break and enter	1008	207	20.5	858	274	31.9
Vehicle theft	448	141	31.4	891	128	14.3
Stealing>K1000	234	66	28.2	309	83	26.8
Fraud>K1000 and misappropriation	78	48	61.5	88	67	76.1
Escape from prison	50	48	96.0	59	91	154.2
Drug offences	303	359	118.0	359	451	125.6
Firearms offences	169	187	110.7	153	199	130.1
Escape from police	93	77	82.7	161	89	55.2
Total	4201	2207	52.5*	5174	2352	5.4**

Notes: *Excluding drug and firearms offences
**Excluding prison escapes and drug and firearms offences
Percentage arrests have been calculated from statistical information from Department of Police.
Source: Royal Papua New Guinea Constabulary.

crime problem is 'directly proportionate to the extent of white-collar crime in the country and outstanding issues concerning public fraud'. He said politicians brought before the leadership tribunal on charges of misappropriation resign from office before being prosecuted, and suspended public servants remain on full pay (*Post-Courier* 7–9 January 2000:6).

Table 2 shows offences and arrests for January to May 1997 and for the same period in 1998. Calculations indicate that arrest rates for drug and firearm offences in both years, and prison escapes in 1998, exceeded the number of offences reported. This is because more opportunities occur during drug and firearm investigations to arrest groups of offenders. Alarmingly, while reports of serious sexual

Table 3 Most prevalent crime reported/recorded and arrests made in National Capital District and nationally, 1 January to 31 December 1997

	National Capital District			Papua New Guinea			Percentage of NCD offences/arrests to national total	
	Offences	Arrests	% arrests	Offences	Arrests	% arrests	% national offences	% national arrests
Robbery	1707	312	18.2	2815	814	28.9	60.6	38.3
Break and enter	874	155	17.7	2433	525	21.5	35.9	29.5
Vehicle theft	1253	155	12.3	1525	172	11.2	82.1	90.1
Serious sexual	360	144	40.0	1392	643	46.1	25.8	37.3
Total	4194	766	18.2	8165	2154	26.3	51.3	35.5

Source: Royal Papua New Guinea Constabulary.

offences, grievous bodily harm/wounding, vehicle theft and stealing rose significantly in 1998, the level of recorded arrests for such offences fell, compared with the same period in 1997. For example, over January to May 1997–98, reported robberies fell by a small percentage but there were 15.3 per cent fewer arrests. Escapes from the police increased by 68 but arrests decreased by 27.5 per cent. The proportion of arrests relating to serious sexual offences, grievous bodily harm and robbery all decreased. These reductions in apprehension may have resulted from increased protection of criminals by communities disillusioned by the criminal justice system. However too much weight should not be given to these trends over a two-year period.

Table 3 compares reported offence and arrests rates for the most prevalent crimes in the NCD and nationally. Importantly it indicates that while NCD is responsible for over half the offences reported and recorded nationally, it accounts for only 35.5 per cent of national arrests—serious sexual offences reported in NCD representing over one-quarter of those reported nationally, robbery at over 60 per cent of national reports and car thefts at 82 per cent of total complaints. The difference in arrest rates between NCD and other provinces could be due to the above mentioned factors relating to access to police stations and police capacity. The higher NCD crime rates relate to overcrowding, youth unemployment, poverty, minimal or no access to land, greater need for cash and other stresses of urban living.

The National Courts

The National Courts have been publishing court statistics in the Annual Reports for judges for some years, but the accidental deletion of the computer data in 1996 reduced the courts' capacity to access information by offence, age and sex. In any case the Office of National Planning and Department of Finance rarely use court statistics, making data collection by National Courts a low priority. District Court records have only allowed manual access, and although computer records are now being produced, returns from provincial courts are irregular, inaccurate or incomplete. This lack of statistics is further hampered by a lack of annual reporting by District Courts. For example, while an Annual Report of the Judges was tabled in Parliament in 1994, the Magisterial Service produced only one Annual Report in 1985 plus an unpublished report (Legal Institutions Strengthening Project [LISP] 1997a:6). There are serious resource implications for such inadequate reporting. Also, the intermittent information sent to politicians and to the community of the performance of National Courts grossly understates the difficulties the criminal justice system is encountering. A Combined Annual Brief for 1996 and 1997 by Lohia Lennie Raka, the Deputy Registrar of Policy and Planning, indicates that a total of 1,777 criminal cases were registered for hearing by the National Courts in 1995, 1,768 cases were registered in 1996 and 1,475 cases were registered in 1997 (these figures include bench warrants, both current and fresh, after committals[1]). Given that the police reported 2,154 arrests in 1997, national courts must have accumulated a considerable backlog of pending criminal cases in that year. Mr Raka believed the backlog could have been caused by factors including the skill level of magistrates in interpreting and applying legislation, lack of consultation with other magistrates and agencies, and poor recording systems and resource deficiencies. In compiling his report, Mr Raka did not consult court users like the RPNGC for information on possible reasons for the fall off of cases in 1997. He suggested however that reasons could include increases in pre-trial standards hence an increase in paperwork, increased cautioning and discontinuance of complaints, low morale, police patrols of areas with high criminality, and a lack of court resources.

In April 1996, it was announced that there were no circuit funds in the A-GD for the rest of that year. This meant that public prosecutors or public solicitor and solicitor-general officers could not travel to provinces, therefore 18 provincial and district centres did not hold circuit courts (LISP 1997a). In June 1998, it was announced that court sittings were delayed by three months because the K26 million budget for judicial services had been reduced substantially. In March 2001, principal magistrates threatened to sue the Judicial and Legal Services Commission for non-payment of K2.8 million in overdue entitlements dating back to 1993, warning that such neglect may result in 'an imminent crisis in the disposal of court cases' (*Post-Courier* 26 June 1998:2, 2–4 March 2001). In October 2001 the Northern Province Provincial Police Commander blamed the absence of a resident judge and infrequent court circuits on long waits in jail for remandees, resulting in frequent escapes (*Post-Courier* 26 October 2001).

The Attorney-General

The A-GD is plagued by the same problems as other criminal justice agencies in relation to data collection, collation and processing. The annual reports file has documents from 1977 to 1989 but thereafter was not kept up. Some internal reports have been prepared however, for example an Annual Management Report in 1995 and a Performance Report for January to June 1997. The A-GD oversees the Parole Board which approves the release from prison of long-term prisoners on Parole Orders. Community correctional officers supervise such orders, an integral part of the rehabilitation of offenders. There has been a lack of regular approval of orders for a long time however, contributing to prison overcrowding and high levels of prisoner anxiety, resulting in frequent escapes. Table 4 indicates the gradual deterioration in the status of parole applications recorded and considered in 1994, 1995 and 1997. In 1996 only 60 per cent of parole applications were granted and in 1997, only 8.1 per cent, leaving 1,030 applications awaiting Board consideration (Borrey and Sabadi 1996:Chart 13).

Statistics from 1997 also indicate that only 35.7 per cent of applicants were granted full release, or were released on licence before parole could be considered (LISP 1997a:6). Provincial magistrates, provincial community correctional officers, and parole board members say the low number of prisoners granted parole is due to the inability of the parole service to provide reports. This is due to the unavailability of vehicles and petrol to travel to prisons to interview prisoners, and to remote locations to interview families of prisoners. To compound this desperate situation, the Parole Board did not have a chairperson for almost two years from 1997 to 1999, creating a further backlog of cases pending. At the end of 1995, only 1,426

Table 4 Parole applications recorded and considered by the Parole Board, 1994, 1995, 1997

Case status	1994	1995	1997
Applications recorded by Board	297	325	2232
Prisoners accepting Board decision	..	..	2024
Parole orders granted	27	10	182
Parole orders refused	34	18	78
Discharge from prison before parole considered	..	..	591
Discharge on licence before parole considered	..	..	208
Escape before parole considered	..	..	9
Applications pending	236	297	1030

Source: Department of Attorney-General.

community based orders—that is probation, parole and community service orders for adults and juveniles—were recorded nationally. In the same year approximately 3,000 break and enters, 500 vehicle thefts, 400 fraudulent offences and 1,200 drug related offences were reported to police (Borrey and Sabadi 1996:Chart 16, LISP 1997a:7). A major conclusion from these statistics is that if prosecutions ensued from such reports to police, many petty offenders were jailed rather than offered community based orders—this due to A-GD's minimal organisational capacity to advise the judiciary on community-based options and to supervise offenders. There is a requirement for community correctional officers to attend court sittings and be available to advise magistrates on community based sentencing, but there is usually only one officer available per province to advise courts, supervise adult and juvenile clients and criminal compensation orders, write pre-sentence and pre-parole reports, train and supervise volunteers, attend to administrative matters and liaise with communities. The best and cheapest long-term, front-end sentencing option to prevent crime and induce behavioural change in petty offenders is community-based supervision—and courts prefer it. Yet there are insufficient resources in place to sustain it; that is, to free up community correctional officers to advise magistates regularly on community-based sentencing options, to write reports on demand,

and to supervise offenders. In the meantime, courts are confined to sentencing petty offenders to jail where they can learn how to become better criminals.

Juvenile offenders

The A-GD is also responsible for the supervision of juvenile offenders, that is youth 17 years and younger, but many are jailed in adult prisons due to inadequate resources. At the end of 1995, there were only 185 males and 8 females in juvenile detention centres (LISP 1997a:7). The situation remains unchanged. There are several reasons for this. The Juvenile Justice Act written in the early 1990s has not been ratified by Parliament and so cannot be enacted by judiciary or by government officials. When sentencing juveniles, magistrates either use the old Juvenile Justice Act that gives few alternatives to incarceration, or use a mixture of the old and new acts—a practise that is not strictly legal. Only those detention centres approved under certain criteria in the old Act can be utilised, limiting the number of beds available for offenders. In any case, magistrates believe some centres are not secure enough for high-risk offenders or associated community-based monitoring is inadequate. Magistrates' access to advice on community-based sentencing options is often dependent upon the availability of a welfare officer from the Department of Home Affairs. The attendance in court of such officers is often affected by lack of departmental resource capacity. Moreover the churches that run juvenile centres have not received government subsidies for years. Consequently some centres have closed, others are run down and insecure, while others have empty beds.

Juvenile incarceration statistics are haphazard. Prison officials estimate that the number of juveniles, mainly boys, incarcerated in adult prisons at any given time, ranges from one to twenty, with higher numbers in regional jails. Most are remanded in custody, instead of given bail, to await court hearings. Others are convicted of petty offences like theft of clothes and food, pick-pocketing or bag snatching—usually attracting prison sentences of several days to three months. For example, Bomana prison recorded admissions of 20 male juveniles remanded in custody awaiting court hearings in

January 1999, and a further 12 male juveniles remanded in custody in February 1999. Over the same two months, only five juveniles were convicted by courts and sentenced to terms of imprisonment at that institution. Although juveniles sleep in separate dormitories in larger jails, they usually share a compound with adult prisoners. In smaller jails where there is no segregation, trusted prisoners are selected to protect juveniles against predatory prisoners. Correctional staff and prisoners say this is not always successful.

Village courts

The A-GD oversees the Village Court Secretariat. Each village court keeps its own records on the number and type of cases heard if stationery is available, and each court reports periodically to the Village Court Secretariat. The village court system comprises over 1,000 courts and 11,000 officials and is an important part of the judicial system. In recent years, village courts have moved from their traditional role of arbitrating minor disputes to dealing with a range of matters, some of which are outside their jurisdiction (LISP 1999). They are plagued with operational problems relating to training and under-resourcing—many officials are unpaid—and there is no money available for supervisory visits to maintain sentencing standards (LISP 1997a). It is not unusual for village courts to hear multiple and varied cases in one sitting. At Baruni village in the NCD in 1998, the village ourt heard up to ten cases a day, comprising stealing, sorcery, assault, property damage and adultery complaints with penalties of either compensation, fines or combinations of both. Village court officials also participate in conciliation regarding tribal fighting, family and community dispute resolution, often resolved through compensation payments.

The prisons

PNGCS statistical records of prisoner intake for 1998 and 1999 are incomplete. Statistics started drying up around August 1998, because of 'no money' for postage to prisons of prisoner statistical registers and no money for prisons to post monthly statistics to headquarters.

Available statistics indicate that while Papua New Guinea has 20 prisons it is rare for more than 17 of them to accept prisoners at any one time. This is because health authorities close prisons periodically due to typhoid outbreaks or other health hazards. PNGCS admittance records indicate that at any one time there are approximately 3,600 prisoners in prisons. Most are adult males between the ages of 18 and 25 jailed for petty offences, unpaid fines or outstanding warrants. Only one-third of prisoners were convicted of violent crime. The official maximum capacity of regional prisons in NCD, Morobe, Madang, Western Highlands and East New Britain provinces is not more than 500, but prison populations often exceed this number. In 1997 over 56 per cent of 11,445 admissions were remand prisoners—languishing in overcrowded cells for up to 12 months awaiting court hearings and sapping meagre jail resources.

Despite a policy of reducing the number of remand prisoners, statistics reveal that remand admissions between January and July 1998 decreased by only 72, compared with the same period in 1997. In August 1999, the late Benedict Kasi, then Commanding Officer of Bomana prison, told the former PNGCS Minister Mathias Karane who was visiting the prison that 'half the prisoners' were on remand. In March 2000, one-quarter of the prisoners at Kerevat prison in East New Britain were on remand and resources there were overstretched. In September 2001, the PNGCS Commissioner said—after the escape of 47 remand prisoners—that 75 per cent of prisoners were on remand costing K2.5 million to feed and keep.

On visits to Bomana prison and to provincial prisons throughout Papua New Guinea, I have been appalled at the overcrowded conditions in which prisoners are made to live: many sleeping crammed on concrete floors; many suffering frequent respiratory infections and outbreaks of infectious diseases such as typhoid. While the Correctional Service Development Project is working with the PNGCS to upgrade buildings and implement maintenance regimes, the situation remains unsatisfactory—prisoners escaping frequently from such conditions aggravated by court and parole board backlogs, jail closures, and the limited capacity of police and the A-GD to monitor bail orders. Parole board hold-ups in 1997 left 1,030 parole applications pending—meaning that 1,030 prisoners eligible for parole consideration remained in jail (LISP 1997a:6). In the Kerevat case, no funds were available to bring a public prosecutor to the province. Table 5 shows how resource deficiencies stall national court sentencing and block community-based supervision possibilities. These deficiencies include lack of knowledge and skill, poor management, administrative problems related to training, and a lack of materials. Political interference, fear of intimidation or loss of allegiance and social and cultural complexities compound such deficiencies.

Women in prison

There are fewer women in jail than men—women comprise less than four per cent of all prisoners. With the exception of some highlands prisons that carry higher female prisoner populations, numbers per prison range from one to twenty females at any given time, while medium and small jails rarely carry more than five. Living conditions and diets in female prisoner compounds are better than those in male compounds. This appears to be for two main reasons: first, cells are not crowded; and second, women are more inclined than men to make gardens, to clean and to cook. Also, women prisoners have greater access to educational programs than men because of their smaller numbers. Church-based organisations, with limited resources, sponsor programs such as Life Skills including family relationships, cooking, craft and literacy. While a constant flow of women are jailed for selling marijuana, stealing, or for prostitution—mainly in an effort to provide livelihoods for their families otherwise unattainable through legitimate means—many women especially in the highlands, are jailed for violent acts that occur in polygamous relationships. These often result in the murder or attempted murder of either the husband or new wife or girlfriend. In mid-2000, at Bomana prison, two women (with their babies) were in custody on remand for killing their mutual husband who brought home a third wife without their consent. In March 1997, at Bomana, a woman sentenced to life imprisonment for killing her husband's new wife told a former PNGCS Minister, Peter Arul, that her husband was implicated in the crime because he failed to secure her consent to the new wife before bringing her home. In November

1997, most of the 40 women prisoners at Baisu prison at Mount Hagen had been convicted of serious assault or murder of either their husbands or their husband's new wives.

A large number of women are also jailed for adultery—a criminal offence in Papua New Guinea—and one for which more women than men are jailed. Village courts often deal with adultery complaints, ordering girlfriends of husbands to pay compensation to the wife or wives. While this may resolve the matter, some wives, fearing diminished resource distribution from their husbands, insist upon imprisonment of the offender as well as compensation. Mount Hagen resident judge, Justice Timothy Hinchcliffe, has taken up these grievances. He believes that men in polygamous relationships, who do not take appropriate responsibility for their wives, should serve half the sentence meted out to the woman who commits a killing (*Post-Courier* 26 June 2001). While such draconian legislation commits more women to jail than need be—sometimes for lengthy periods—a senior female prison official, noted for her humanitarian views and creative management style, said female prisoners unlike many male prisoners, benefit from their time in jail. This is because they are released from some very bad domestic violence situations and have the time and freedom to learn and to 'be themselves'.

The weak state and law and order

Papua New Guinea is a 'weak' state; that is, a state that does not comply with policy and legislation. Its legitimacy is undermined by a fragile legal and regulatory framework, minimum institutional capacity, poor and deteriorating service delivery, poor planning and budget structures, low accountability, and endemic corruption. These problems make administration of justice non-transparent, unaccountable and liable to political involvement. Papua New Guinea citizens and international donors believe widespread corruption within government circles is the root cause of the country's under-development and crime problems—stripping from public coffers vast earnings of natural resources—wastage and 'insatiable avarice'

Table 5 Inhibitors to national court sentencing

Inhibitors to sentencing	Impacts on criminal justice system
Pre-trial standards and paperwork deficiencies in: police investigation techniques, police interviewing/ recording techniques, prosecution preparation and presentation, probation officer pre-sentence reports.	Sentencing delays. Imbalanced sentencing. Defendants remanded in custody for lengthy periods. Time delays and scarce custodial resources prisoner remand periods. Reduced credibility of criminal justice agencies.
Low morale, due, for example, to poor housing, poor remuneration, few work tools/resources no recognition for good work or training.	Absenteeism. Inadequate supervision. Inaccurate and/or irregular statistics. Unavailability of statistics and reports. Time delays and scarce custodial resources impacting on prisoner remand periods. Reduced credibility of criminal justice agencies.
Lack of resources, for example: no stationery or typewriters/ photocopiers to produce reports, no vehicles, or petrol for vehicles, to conduct interviews to produce reports, or transport prisoners to court, no funds to transport the judiciary, public prosecutors, or public defenders to court hearings, inadequately skilled human resources.	Insufficient capacity to cope with demands. Inability to conduct interviews for court reports. Inability to produce prisoners for court hearings. Inability to conduct court hearings in remote locations. Inability of inadequately skilled staff to interpret legislation and recommend appropriate sentencing to the judiciary. Time delays and scarce custodial resources impacting on prisoner remand periods. Reduced credibility of criminal justice agencies.

Poor execution by magistrates: not recording reasons for sentencing, not interpreting/applying legislation correctly, not consulting one another regarding sentencing.	Reduced future balanced sentencing opportunities. Reduced effectiveness of future prosecutions. Increased future incidents of inappropriate sentencing of recidivists for similar offences. Reduced credibility of judiciary. Time delays and scarce custodial resources impacting on prisoner remand periods.
Influence of local environments and *wantok*ism on sentencing, for example: Political or social obligations of magistrates or other criminal justice agency officials in relation to a defendant or a case, fear of intimidation or loss of allegiance if demands are not met, local social mores and expectations of punishment may erupt into violence against criminal justice agency officials if expectations are not met.	Reduced standardised sentencing. Reduced credibility of criminal justice agencies. Political, social, and economic repercussions due to lack of impartiality of judiciary. Continuance of intimidation, violence and corruption.
Minimal links by courts to other government and non-government agencies, for example: the judiciary may be unaware, if not advised of rehabilitative educational and awareness programs for offenders that may be more appropriate than custodial sentences.	Unnecessary custodial sentences for minor offences. Increased strain on scarce custodial resources. Delayed offender rehabilitation. Reduced credibility of judiciary.

Source: National Registry, Department of Justice.

resulting in the loss of public confidence in state run criminal justice systems and a significant reduction in state capacity to control crime (Mohan 1996, Chan Kin-hung 1996, Torres 1996). Sir Anthony Siaguru of Transparency International (PNG) said corruption in Papua New Guinea is 'like a cancer chewing into the fabric of society and slowly eroding established norms of doing business'. He lamented the laxity of officials unless paid off, misuse of public monies and assets for personal gain, appointment of cronies of politicians to public office, and the running down of once productive and independent government institutions (Siaguru 2000c). Another commentator is Helen Hughes, a professor emeritus from The Australian National University, and guest speaker at the jointly-sponsored Institute of National Affairs and Transparency International, Privatisation and the Integrity Pact forum held in Port Moresby on 28 February 2000. Hughes told the forum that Papua New Guinea is one of the worst performing countries in the world—consumption decreasing by one per cent per year since 1980, and social indicators amongst the worst in the world—especially literacy, maternal health and infant mortality. Hughes compared resource-rich Papua New Guinea, receiving copious amounts of aid, with land locked Botswana—a country with few natural resources whose economy has grown at 7.5 per cent per year over the last decade. She said international donors are becoming tired of complaints from Papua New Guinea, high expectations of handouts with few returns, and the blaming of foreigners for the country's woes. What can be done and how quickly? When opening the forum, Prime Minister Morauta said, 'turning the nation around is like trying to turn a huge oil tanker travelling at speed. If the master turns the course too sharply it may capsize'. He reiterated the analogy in November 2000 when he announced the adjournment of Parliament for six months to avoid a no-confidence vote and downfall of his government.

The people's expectations of criminal justice agencies to combat crime are high, but like other government agencies, they are caught within a complex network of political invasions, corruption and obligatory networks. Politicisation of the administration of justice presents one of the gravest threats to state legitimacy and operation (Dinnen 1999). Such interference and consistent under-resourcing of criminal justice agencies has resulted in reactionary, unpredictable and inconsistent behaviour to meet political agendas—all characteristics of a weak state. In an effort to provide a strong, accountable, legal and regulatory framework, a number of important offices of government were set up under the PNG Constitution. They are, the legislature (the National Parliament), the Executive (the Prime Minister and his Cabinet Ministers and the Departments that come under them) and the Judiciary (the Courts). The Constitution also established other important bodies and protected them from change or control by Acts of Parliament by the government of the day. These bodies are the RPNGC, the PNGDF, the Ombudsman Commission, the Office of the Auditor-General, the Office of the Public Prosecutor, the Officer of the Public Solicitor and the Electoral Commission. The role of the RPNGC is defined in Section 197 of the Constitution: to preserve peace and good order and to maintain and as necessary enforce the law in an impartial and objective manner. While the NEC can, through the Police Minister, direct the police force to maintain law and order, no one external to the police force can direct police members to arrest, charge or prosecute any persons. The independence of the Offices of the Public Prosecutor and Public Solicitor are also protected. The role of the Public Prosecutor is to prosecute people accused of committing a serious crime and that of the Public Solicitor is to assist citizens accused of a crime and the public generally with legal problems (Nonggorr 1998b). A risk to the independence of criminal justice agencies is that the NEC appoints departmental and divisional heads. As a result public service leaders often bow to political pressure for fear of losing their jobs and make decisions that favour the government of the day rather than the public good (*Post-Courier* 21 February 2000:10). The Chief Secretary, Robert Igara, said it is common for government Ministers to threaten public servants, to interfere in public service decisions and to make decisions that go against their own laws. The PNG Business Council told the 12th Papua New Guinea–Australia Ministerial Forum held in Port Moresby on 10 March 2000, that public servants are afraid to do their work because of political interference and this affects service delivery (Papua New Guinea Institute of National Affairs Speech

Series 9 February 2000, Hiambohn 2000a).

There has been a 'do nothing' approach by criminal justice agency leaders when opportunities arise for them to make unpopular decisions to deflect cronyism that affects staff promotions and transfers and to redress the improper use of public monies in agency trust accounts. While a more reliable audit process appears to be emerging, the long-term result of the 'do nothing' approach is that stalemates distress agency staff and frustrate aid agency workers. Perceived weak leadership also undermines the personal integrity of leaders and the integrity of the office. A senior PNGCS officer, who had waited hours to see a divisional head who failed to keep the appointment told me 'I respect the office', the connotation being 'I do not respect the person in the office'. The general view is that such politicians and heads of government departments are caught up in what Sir John Kaputin describes as the 'power-minority that engages in the crude politics of exploiting the hopes of people who are genuinely poor and needy'. Sir John believes the unprecedented scale on which 'orderly, established procedures are disregarded' in preparation and implementation of the Budget in economic management and in the way Cabinet meetings are called or deferred, has resulted in increased unplanned expenditure and a drastic fall in international confidence in the commitment of PNG leaders to good governance (Kaputin 1999). Weak leadership creates opportunities for corruption. Criminal justice agency staff take advantage of such weakness and of poorly maintained administrative systems to gain benefits. Citizens express sympathy for under-resourced criminal justice agencies, but they also express anger and despair when they experience abuse from drunken and disorderly criminal justice officers and witness the blatant misuse of government vehicles for drinking binges and family excursions. Most people do not speak out because whistleblowers tend to suffer swift, merciless physical punishment, property destruction, sackings or transfers. Understandably, many criminal justice staffers are 'too scared to speak out' (*Post-Courier* 2 February 2000:10).

The judiciary attempts to restore public confidence by prosecuting perpetrators when there are resources to collect sufficient evidence. For example, when four Lae policemen were fined more than K1,500 for assaulting members of the public and breaching the peace, Magistrate Jerry Singomat told them they 'must step in line in [their] own boundaries' and be accountable to the public (*Post-Courier* 3 January 2000:7). Occasionally leaders are jailed for misappropriation and other criminal behaviour, but frequently, insufficient evidence prevents prosecution. An example is the discharge in March 2001 of the Skate insurance fraud case. Many allegations of fraud by political and other leaders are never prosecuted. For example, the *Post-Courier* (9 March 2000:3) reported that the government was instituting recovery proceedings against those who benefited from the K18 million Cairns Conservatory deal. The scam involved several members of the previous government. Despite these pronouncements no one has as yet been prosecuted.

The Prime Minister said when opening the February 2000 Privatisation and Integrity Pact forum in Port Moresby, that public sector structural reform is the long-term, sustainable way to create attitudinal and behavioural change protecting, strengthening and, where necessary, modifying legislation and policy and systems. With a view to debating political and other issues, the PNG Institute of National Affairs initiated regular public forums in February 2000. At the first of the forums the Chief Secretary, Robert Igara said the approved reform agenda would establish systems of management and accountability to allay fears, restore integrity, create consistency, engender donor and investor trust and confidence and enhance international perception of Papua New Guinea. To facilitate this a parliamentary committee, called the Central Agencies Committee and led by Mr Igara, was formed to coordinate and monitor policy, financial discipline and process. Reforms have been designed to create ownership by citizens of the process of public administration and include strategies to enable the NEC to drive and prioritise decisions, adhere to proper process and create budget discipline. Mr Igara believes the key to ownership of appropriate change is participation, and both citizens and expatriates are responsible for this. He acknowledged that there is no quick fix solution and positive change takes time, patience and commitment. He emphasised that unless 'we have fundamental political requirements nothing can happen'. 'Requirements' include legislative reform especially in relation to the

Organic Law and changes to the electoral system. The latter includes replacing first-past-the-post voting by proportional representation to encourage stable, cooperative and cohesive governance for more than two years—hopefully with the same Ministers in the same portfolios. The Organic Law was originally designed to decentralise administration and give more powers and participation to communities. One reason this is not occurring is that provincial administrations have become over-centralised and politicised because government Ministers head provincial or district committees in their home provinces. Hearsay suggests that bribes are frequent amongst criminal justice agency staff to waive apprehension and prosecution, lose files, distort the procurement process or steal government equipment. Mr Igara believes this practice may be deterred by Central Agencies Commitee working closely with the Financial Management Committee to oversee, formulate and implement departmental annual plans that link with budgetary requirements and structural reform including privatisation, departmental performance and investigation, and with arbitration of disputes.

Patience, time and commitment are needed to implement reforms. This is because some managers are deficient in skills demanded by the modern work environment, or are too pre-occupied with their own interests to implement policy effectively. Some managers spend much time on personal *bisnis* or on devising political strategies for personal gain or protection. The result is that staff do not experience satisfying learning environments and tend to mirror the behaviour of their aberrant managers. Some managers have difficulty interpreting and applying the legislation under which they work. One reason for this is that Public Service Guidelines agreed to in 1976 were not published until 1994, and there has been little or no follow up training. An expressed loss of faith in leadership is common. One prison commander told me in 1999 that he had no faith in the ability of senior headquarters staff and would prefer them not to come to his prison. Another prison commander said the way to achieve positive organisational change is to 'get rid of the deadwood' in the Executive. Divisional heads hardly communicate with their staff, except to bark an order, or castigate them for wrongdoing. Communication rarely occurs across divisions and then through a cycle of endless memos. Bored, directionless, disillusioned staff play computer games for most of the day or wander around inside and outside the office chatting, smoking and chewing betel nut, or using government vehicles to conduct private business. An Evaluation Report on 'Progress in Prison Industry Pilot Projects' stated that PNGCS staff lack information, are given few incentives and little recognition for good work done and morale and productivity is generally low (Pitts 1999d:9). Correctional officers say 'They [the bosses—with some exceptions] promote their own *wantoks*', '...give us no work briefs', '...no recognition when we work well', '...do not discipline the lazy ones', '...are never here', '...shout at us when there is a problem', '...are always talking, talking but never doing anything'.

In 2001, there is a new PNGCS Commissioner and a new Executive team comprising officers of integrity (*Post-Courier* 13 July 2001:3). Their appointments promise a boost to morale and productivity and are timely in view of the government's structural reform program. Their priority must be to address the lack of basics in prisons; for example, adequate food, adequate health care, hygienic accommodation and consistent prisoner rehabilitation programs. However, resource deficiencies, and an over-taxing of meagre resources by prison overcrowding will stall action. To make any sustainable progress, management must involve the whole organisation in cultural and structural change. To do this, PNGCS must become a learning organisation that recognises quality interactions between management and staff as a core strategy to positive change and progress. This means keeping staff informed, following up on management strategies consistently, and trouble-shooting problems as they occur. The basis of achieving such quality is to ensure management understands legislation, how to apply it in daily settings, and can communicate its application to staff. There has been some considerable progress in this area. For example, in 1997 few prison commanders attended regional legislative training workshops sponsored by AusAID, no executive team members attended and staff attendees received no guidance to apply legislation in daily practice. Practice and procedure manuals were stored in the offices of senior managers and staff training college personnel and most staff had no access to them. In any case, most managers did not believe it was their role to train staff in manual content. In March 1999, I worked with counterparts to facilitate sessions on legislation and practice and procedure at a PNGCS professional development workshop for commanding officers. Many senior officers had neither read nor understood the legislation under which they worked. In 2001, however a PNGCS training team working with the Correctional Service Development Project, has rectified the situation. Local orders have been written and a concerted national effort has been made to train commanding officers and their staff. The continued implementation of such strategy will require recognition of the value and understanding of local orders by management. Training is expensive and continued implementation will require continuous resource provision. To maintain provision at an adequate level, the cost-effectiveness of best practice prison management will need to be reinforced with the Department of Finance.

Ongoing training too, must be sensitive to the literacy levels of recipients. The inertness of some senior PNGCS officers may be a result of their low levels of English literacy. This deficiency is of major concern generally because Papua New Guinea's Constitution, laws and regulations, based on the Westminster model, are written in English. Readers not proficient in this language cannot interpret its full meaning, nor accept and own the values expressed through it. One of the critical components of communication is the way people use and interpret language, and many innovations do not succeed due to poor levels of communication (Kaye 1992, Print 1993). Therefore, while legislation, policies, practice and procedures written in English are developed and reports written in English are distributed on the subjects of structural reforms, management initiatives and systems of accountability, many public servants either cannot read English well enough to interpret and apply the concepts or they find the phraseology completely inhibiting. Managers, deficient in English, write disjointed and illegible reports, horde files, circulars and other information and deny staff access to them. As a consequence little informed debate occurs. A common remark from field staff when something goes wrong is 'I was only following [verbal] instructions'.

Such ignorance of written laws and lack of written instructions reduces state capacity to perform daily tasks and further erodes the reputation and effectiveness of state law and order agencies. Concerns have also been raised about the level of comprehension and interpretation of laws of Legal Training Institute graduates and the poor English literacy levels of arresting police officers and police prosecutors who prepare court briefs and prosecution documents. This results in inadequate presentations and court delays (LISP 1997). Even tertiary educated practitioners read little and display minimal comprehension of written concepts. They argue they do not have time to read as their scarce skills are in high demand. A PNGCS commanding officer expressed his 'disgust' that reports sent to headquarters are neither read nor responded to. Corroborating this, Robert Igara stated during the February 2000 PNG Institute of National Affairs forum 'many senior public servants do not read reports'.

English literacy is essential to create a favourable political and socio-economic environment, to induce positive change and to reduce corrupt behaviour by increasing public awareness to rights and institutionalised procedures. The Singapore Government achieved 91 per cent literacy in 1992 (increasing from 52.3 per cent in 1957) through their adult education program (Mohan 1996:76–7). The UN Development Programme 1997 Human Development Report defines literacy as the ability of people aged 15 and above, to read and write, with understanding, a short, simple statement on their everyday life in a particular language. This definition is inadequate as a person's ability to communicate in a particular language may be confined to his or her social experience and interests, and communication relating to broader concepts expressed in that language may be beyond his or her ken. In Papua New Guinea in 1995, an average of only 29.1 per cent of an estimated average of 45.1 per cent of persons 'totally literate' were literate in English (National Statistical Office 1995:18) In 1999, not more than 52 per cent were considered literate. The ability of 'literate' leaders and public servants to interpret and apply democratic principles and values expressed in English and the ability of PNG citizens to be fully aware of their rights and obligations is therefore questionable.

Papua New Guinea citizens expect their elected government and delegates to keep them informed, to involve them in decision making and to provide adequate goods and services to enhance their educational, economic and social opportunities. They express anguish at a politically influenced and corrupt public sector, effectively denying citizens the 'right of equal access to public service' (*Post-Courier* 10 December 1998:20–1). When such marginalisation occurs, communities turn in on themselves to solve their problems linking with the *bisnis* of politics when a member from their clan or interest group is in power at either provincial or national level. This creates a continuous and cyclical series of relationships and events that distorts resource distribution, condones corrupt practice and cronyism and undermines all efforts to establish systems of accountability for the common good. Autocratic, under-resourced and corrupt governments dominate disillusioned, powerless and poor communities through bureaucratic rules, regulations and contracts. Disincentives, exploitation and corruption occur in both community and government sectors resulting in political instability, low productivity, imbalanced distribution of goods and services and hence diminished investor confidence and donor agency support. Unhealthy co-dependencies occur and are maintained between politicians and communities and the public sector continues to be inefficient and corrupt, creating further imbalance in resource distribution. The private sector loses confidence, investment declines and this contributes to more unemployment. The informal sector remains under-developed, communities become disillusioned, fearful and remain poor and powerless. Politicians in profitable allegiances become richer, creating arrangements that protect their interests and ignoring rules that do not. Crime rises, involves broader socio-economic groups and becomes more sophisticated and harder to control. Desperate communities create their own mechanisms of social order while the government—having already lost control—enacts draconian legislation like the death penalty, uses pillage and burn techniques in an attempt to control communities through fear, further destroying public confidence, and continues to inefficiently dominate rules, regulations and contracts—and the cycle reinforces itself.

This cycle of relationships and events can be seen in PNG criminal justice agencies whose officers have several lines of allegiance. Officially, their allegiance priorities are to the state, to their organisation, to their families and communities. In reality, allegiances are in reverse, priority given to families and communities, then to organisations, then to the state. When under attack, scrutiny or criticism as a result of following a certain political or socio-economic course, lines of allegiance to the state and to organisations are more likely to be abandoned before lines of allegiance to families and communities. Allegiance priorities can cause considerable conflict of interest for personnel when their organisations tell them their core business is to control crime and protect the nation while their communities pressure them to be partial on certain matters. For example, a man who is a policeman between 8.00 am and 4.00 pm may have extended families living in villages in the Western Highlands Province (WHP) and the East Sepik Province, an uncle in the WHP Provincial Government, WHP cousins in a Port Moresby squatter settlement and a brother in jail. The policeman may be married to a woman from Morobe Province who is a correctional service officer, whose father is in the PNGDF and whose brother is a politician. The man may have gone to school with students from the East Sepik, Madang, Sandaun, Western Highlands and Enga Provinces. At school he may have aligned himself with mainly East Sepik students. He may have trained with a mixed group from the Southern Highlands Province, Eastern Highlands Province (EHP) and northern coastal regions and he lives in a barracks community of fellow police officers from all over Papua New Guinea. According to particular interests at particular times, his first allegiance is to one of those interest groups. From time to time the interest groups conflict with one another and that of the police force. To compound this complexity of allegiances, police, prosecutors, state solicitors, court officials and correctional and community correctional officers are deployed to different political, social and economic environments throughout the country, frequently marrying into local communities. These environments can either enhance or inhibit their work, as unity of purpose is often plagued by a multitude of value systems, cultural perspectives, new political alliances, work ethics and styles. As an analogy, pig production is valued and practised differently throughout Papua New Guinea. A Papuan from Rigo cares for pigs differently from an Eastern Highlander from Okapa or a villager from Rabaul. Each has his or her view and experience of raising pigs and each practice is successful in its own environment. A PNGCS commanding officer told me that despite this diversity of experience, perspectives and practice and the presence of new methods, 'traditional ways of doing things' still strongly influences the viability of crime control initiatives by formal agencies, and sometimes renders them unfeasible. The 'traditional' approach, whatever the perception of 'tradition' is, is the best. 'We do things in our own way…'. Prisons are located in different environments and 'what may work in one prison may not necessarily work in another' (Pitts 1999d:11). With a view to adapting to the values, expectations and needs of local environments, each criminal justice agency develops its own sub-culture to enable members to live harmoniously. For example, the RPNGC and the PNGCS sub-cultures in the EHP may differ from police and PNGCS sub-cultures in ENB, and again from similar groups in the NCD. Different sub-cultures developed have a huge impact on the 'ways things are done', 'what is done' and 'what is not done' in each environment. Historically, initiatives and procedures developed external to local environments—without the agreement of, and participation with, communities—are often discarded, leaving aid agencies like AusAID wondering how projects they have funded have failed. In relation to controlling crime, generic laws and procedure developed without consultation and participation by communities, including local criminal justice communities, are not valued, and if applied are rarely applied consistently. Given that criminal justice agency personnel are themselves caught up in the social and political environments in which they live and work, it is understandable that their approach to state dictates of social control, in relation to which they may not have been consulted, is often piecemeal and selective.

Papua New Guinea has a pluralistic legal system: customary systems of law co-exist with an introduced one (Larmour 1998). The country also has robust criminal laws, but its criminal justice system is often undermined by a distrust of its application. On 1 March 2000, the *Post-Courier* reported that a lawyer had been '...jostled and objects thrown at him and his vehicle kicked and punched...' by a group of complainants in relation to a particular court case, because they did not 'respect the rule of law'. The same newspaper reported Chief Justice, and Chairman of the Legal Training Institute Council Sir Justice Amet, as saying, '...in a free society under the rule of law, the function of the legislature is to create and maintain conditions which uphold the dignity of an individual...his civil and political rights...social, economic, educational and cultural conditions...essential to the full development of his personality'. Justice Amet also stated that '...the rule of law depends [upon] the provision of adequate safeguards against abuse of power by the Executive and...an effective government capable of maintaining law and order...ensuring adequate social and economic conditions...', and '...except subject to an Act of Parliament to the contrary...nobody may be convicted of an offence that is not defined by...and prescribed by a written law' and must '...be allowed to appear [before a Court] and be heard on the matter in question...' (Amet 2000:3). The reported 'jostling' of a lawyer doing his job is not only an indication of a lack of respect for and knowledge of state laws but also an indication of a lack of knowledge of the process within which a constitutional democracy is bound to work to preserve such laws. Criminal justice agencies are front line agencies delegated with legislative knowledge and responsibility to educate communities about laws and their rights and obligations to maintain peace and good order. Educating communities including criminal justice communities about laws, due process, rights and obligations is crucial to maintaining peace and good order. Papua New Guinea citizens say they want to work with criminal justice agencies and agency officers say they want to work more closely with communities when resources allow. While many citizens say they prefer community courts to arbitrate local disputes and grievances, they also say they expect state law and order agencies to lead, train and support their decision making. When criminal justice agencies cannot fulfil this role, disillusionment occurs and communities take steps to maintain order in ways that may not be sanctioned by the state.

Conclusion

This chapter has emphasised that crime is Papua New Guinea's single biggest deterrent to business investment, to tourism and to political, social and economic growth. Crime in Papua New Guinea is well organised and orchestrated and is rarely altruistic. Sophisticates and specialised criminals lead uneducated and financially deprived youth in criminal networks allegedly linked with political and government circles through reciprocity arrangements that provide mutual benefits. Many crimes victimise the poor, old, young and vulnerable and the perceived increasing viciousness of crime and violence against women negates the excuse 'I did it because I was hungry'. Domestic violence is rampant, often tragic and increasing; ethnic bias prompts violent crimes manifesting in frequent killings, muggings, rapes and clan warfare. Less than half of the crime reported results in the arrest—let alone prosecution—of offenders.

Statistics kept by criminal justice agencies are notoriously unreliable or unavailable because they are not reported or recorded regularly or accurately. Available statistics do nevertheless suggest enormous increases in reported crime especially serious sexual offences, robbery, car theft, prison escapes and drug and firearm-related offences. National Capital District accounts for over half the offences reported and arrests are low. Statistics reveal court and parole board backlogs, inadequate resources for juvenile detention centres and problematic operations of village courts. These cause considerable stress on prison populations and resources resulting in frequent escapes. Women devoid of education, ignorant of their social and economic rights and deprived of legitimate economic opportunities are thrust into prostitution, marijuana dealing, theft and commit crimes of passion in frustration. The weak legal and regulatory framework of the PNG Government, deteriorating service delivery, poor planning and budget structures and little commitment to accountability, reduce the capacity of law enforcers to apprehend, prosecute, sentence and contain offenders—trying the patience and commitment of international donors. Law and order agencies, caught between public expectations and a maze of obligatory relationships and political agendas, are selective rather than effective in controlling crime, further reducing opportunity costs of committing crime and inadvertently legitimising community crime controls.

Review of the electoral system and public sector structural reform appear to be the key to increased accountability and encouragement of consistent, transparent governance. However, while senior public servants participate in corrupt practices do not read reports, do not participate in the process of change and do not lead and educate their staff and the general public in reforms, the success of the touted reform process is problematic. Reform may also be jeopardised if appropriate learning environments that allow workers and the general public to understand and absorb change are not created. Moreover, women are excluded from change management decision making and democratic principles are ignored.

Note

1 Bench warrants, in this instance, are warrants issued by judges during court proceedings for the arrest of a person who has failed to appear in relation to a court case that has been committed for hearing to a higher court, such as the District Court, by the Magistrates Court. Offences considered to be more serious than others, according to certain criteria, are committed for hearing in higher courts. The inclusion of current and fresh bench warrants in the annual number of cases registered for hearing at courts can distort statistics in relation to fresh cases registered for hearing.

4
Criminal justice agency crime prevention efforts and the impact of Australian aid inputs

It has long been recognised that governments are neither all-powerful nor all-competent to prevent and control crime—the manifestation of a combination of social and economic grievances, perceived benefits and reduced opportunity costs—and criminal law is only a small part of a social engine designed to provide peace and good order (Grabosky 1996, Campos 1997). Considered in this context, formal criminal justice agencies can be only one element in crime prevention and control.

Criminal justice agency crime prevention efforts

Papua New Guinea criminal justice agencies flounder in dealing with prevalent crime and the challenge of balancing the introduced Westminster legal system with the underlying law according to 'custom'. Before and since Independence there have been crime summits, reports on law and order and prevention strategies, the framing of draconian legislation like the death penalty, punitive prison sentences and the introduction of boom gates, curfews, raids and roadblocks. The RPNGC, PNGCS and A-GD have developed corporate plans with visions, missions and goals. The RPNGC has a Code of Ethics and expects each member to exhibit fairness, honesty, respect, excellence, confidentiality, discipline, morality, accountability and acceptance towards one another and the general public. The A-GD has adopted core values relating to development, access to law and justice, respect for the law, accountability, equality, the national interest, transparency, international and regional obligations and a custom-founded justice system (RPNGC Strategic Plan 1997–2001, RPNGC Corporate Plan 1997–2001, PNGCS Corporate Plan 1999–2001, A-GD Corporate Plan 1998–2001).

The RPNGC Corporate Plan states that to achieve the mission of 'securing a safer community' police must 'gain the confidence of the peoples of Papua New Guinea…satisfying the needs and gaining the respect of the community through strategies to preserve law and order, community policing, good leadership and accountability, better management of infrastructure, human resources and finance' (RPNGC Corporate Plan 1997–2001:5–6). The PNGCS mission is to 'enhance the protection and wellbeing of society'. Its Corporate Plan and Corporate Goals focus on humane containment and rehabilitation of offenders, setting positive behavioural standards, effecting quality financial management, providing staff with training opportunities and conducive living and working conditions to achieve goals and working with other agencies and communities to provide service (PNGCS Corporate Plan 1999–2001:7–10). The A-GD's mission is to 'develop, provide and promote legal, justice and corporate services to the state for and on behalf of the People of Papua New Guinea'. The Department attempts to achieve this by providing professional legal advice and representation, protecting the interests of state, community and individual, delivering legal, justice and corporate services, promoting participation and partnership, and strengthening institutional capacity. The Secretary and Attorney-General Michael Gene stated in the foreword of the Corporate Plan that it 'sets our vision for the future…and provides the framework...to identify critical policy areas...and prioritise allocation of resources...'. The Minister for Justice in 1999, Jacob Wama stated in his contribution to the Plan that its success 'will not only be measured by how comfortable employees are...and how many new cars we have...but should translate to measure impact on specific areas of service' (A-GD Draft Corporate Plan 1999:1–2). Papua New Guinea is a weak state, however, and lacks the political will, capacity and understanding of agency needs, goals, operational styles and environments to achieve effective social control. State weakness is largely responsible for the current problems permeating criminal justice agencies and manifesting in financial and management deficiencies that lead to poor working and living conditions, minimal discipline, low productivity and confusion regarding roles and responsibilities (Dinnen 1998). The Indian criminal justice system experiences similar difficulties to those in Papua New Guinea. There is a lack of political will to link reforms with resources and to solve enormous problems within time frames that are in conflict with operational demands. Indian police have little or no control over the causes of disorder because they are of a socio-political nature requiring broader political solutions and an understanding of democratic values in a plural society. Police crime prevention efforts are ineffective, and as conflicts increase, police become more authoritarian and less service-oriented. The judiciary, which plays a key role in re-socialising offenders by determining guilt or innocence and imposing punishments and correctional strategies, is hampered by a lack of political and material capacity (Kumar 1997).

In Papua New Guinea, police often react violently to transgressions of state law, courts either fail to sit or they sentence petty offenders to prison—contributing to prison overcrowding—and custodial and community correctional rehabilitation strategies fail. During police crackdowns criminals simply change their patterns of behaviour. For example during curfews, criminals change their operational patterns to rob and pillage by day rather than by night. Reports of police brutality are common. Settlement families report violent police raids during which their possessions are destroyed or stolen. Innocent people are killed and injured in the crossfire of police shootouts with criminals, or are run over during high-speed car chases. An elderly man I know, an innocent bystander at a street fight, was upended by police and kicked with steel capped boots, receiving abrasions and bruising. When he reached for his spectacles that had fallen from his pocket, a policeman ground them into the dirt with his boot. In May 1998, I saw police punch and kick a man outside the Badili police station in Port Moresby. They pushed him headlong into the police station and I later heard cries from inside the building. Stories of police harassment at licence and vehicle registration roadblocks are common. One couple had guns pointed at them by drunken officers, and in another incident, a female driver was threatened with jail because her car safety sticker was out of date. Meanwhile rusty cars, trucks and buses overloaded with people, continue to crawl crab-like on Port Moresby roads devoid of head and taillights, spewing black smoke and in obvious need of major repair.

In August 1998, I experienced a police crowd control operation outside the Goroka Showgrounds. The purpose of the operation was to stop youths scaling the showground fence. I was kneeling in front of a face painter having a blue butterfly painted on my cheek. Suddenly the crowd cleared around me and I was almost neck to jowl with a huge black German shepherd dog, pulling a riot squad policeman behind him. My adrenalin heaved me up just in time to miss the force of the animal and his handler who kicked away the face painter's stand and those of other vendors along the fence. On 5 April 2000, it was reported that auxiliary police had terrorised women vendors at a mini-market at Gerehu in Port Moresby, driving their truck over the women's produce and stealing and eating what was not damaged (Gerawa 2000). The National Capital District Commission had banned street vendors, confining all marketing to designated sites but the women had established their own market because they said the NCD Commission markets were dirty and never cleaned. In November 2001, police attending a burning supermarket in Port Moresby fired warning shots to disperse a crowd of looters, then entered the shop and stole cartons of beer and mattresses. When the crowd saw what the police had done, they shouted at and stoned the police and their vehicles, receiving more warning shots in response (*Post-Courier* 2 November 2001:5).

While PNG citizens abhor some state crime control methods, their expectations of criminal justice agencies to control crime are high. Government spending on law and order, as a percentage of total expenditure, has been less than one per cent. The low level of funding reduces agency capacity to meet demands and to compete with a flourishing crime industry that is better led, better organised, and is a more reliable provider to citizens than is the government (Hunt et al. 1999, Levantis and Chand 1997). While there appeared to be considerable budgetary increase for prisons and police in 1997 and 1998, the 1998 RPNGC allocation as a percentage of recurrent spending was 0.8 per cent less than in 1997 while the PNGCS allocation as a percentage of recurrent spending was only 0.4 per cent more. Allocations to the judiciary as a percentage of recurrent spending remain unchanged over four years at only 0.6 per cent of the recurrent budget while, over the same period, financial support to traditional tribunals fell to only 0.1 per cent of the recurrent budget in 1999. In 2001, while 8.9 per cent of budget allocations was shared by law and order agencies, much of it repaid accumulated debts and met salaries and wages before operational expenditure could be considered.

In 1997, the A-GD had 71 funded staff including 46 field officers, 25 headquarters officers, 13 support staff and 252 volunteers to supervise cases. The department was allocated K1,086,700 in that year, of which K1,050,200 paid for salaries, wages and grants to juvenile institutions. The balance of K36,500 was woefully insufficient to run the department, hence there was inadequate provision of poorly maintained provincial office accommodation, and staff housing was limited. Moreover, there was no money for vehicles and little for office equipment and furniture (LISP 1997:2). In 1998, the annual budget allocation to the A-GD was less than one million kina, insufficient to pay salaries and wages, maintain vehicles, buy stationery, train volunteer supervisors, write reports and conduct inspection tours. In 1999, community correctional officers were working in appalling conditions with poor lighting, no office equipment, no vehicles and no telephones. One community correctional officer not only had an outstanding expense tally for stationery and other items, but also had not been paid for months. He had sought help from the provincial government but had been referred back to the A-GD. Other community correctional officers related similar experiences; one was particularly distressed by not being able to run a three-day course for volunteer supervisors.

The Organic Law on provincial governments and local-level governments states that a public authority must be adequately resourced to perform its functions and that the Provincial and District Administrator must supervise and direct all officers and employees assigned or otherwise employed to carry out the functions of the national government—other than the law enforcement agencies unless by special arrangement with these agencies (Government of PNG 1996). In an effort to have provincial governments take responsibility for their share of national government department expenses in their provinces, Memoranda of Understanding were signed by criminal justice agencies and provincial governments in early 1999. In June 1999, some provincial governments had honoured their commitments, providing materials to maintain prison infrastructure. Other provincial governments said financial allocations from the national government were insufficient to extend to local criminal justice agencies and believed that these should remain a national responsibility.

With little or no responsibility being taken by either national or provincial governments, inadequate resource provision continues to cripple the capacity of criminal justice agencies. For the A-GD, it means a lack of funds for stationery, equipment and vehicles and a stalling of a range of activities by community correctional officers including researching and writing pre-sentence and pre-parole reports, travelling to prisons and communities to interview prisoners and their families, conducting training programs for volunteers, supervising volunteers, inspecting juvenile institutions and attending courts, conferences and training programs. The result is that community-based order eligible prisoners are held in custody longer, which overcrowds prisons, overstretches resources and inhibits rehabilitative efforts in contravention of basic human rights. For the PNGCS, it meant that, for a large part of 1999, telephones at headquarters and at several prisons were disconnected for non-payment of accounts—in fact few prisons have constant telephone and fax communication—and water and power supplies are regularly disconnected for non-payment of bills or for other reasons. Moreover, there is never enough money for prisoner food, medical supplies, vehicle maintenance, diesel and stationery. Long delays in payment by PNGCS to provincial transport depots means that provincial prisons, all situated some distance from towns, cannot obtain fuel on credit and experience considerable difficulty in getting prisoners to courts or collecting supplies from towns. This situation affects the operations of Barawagi prison in Simbu Province in particular, whose telephone lines were sabotaged some years ago over land claims, compelling staff to spend two half-days each week driving to Mount Hagen to collect mail and messages. One prison commander said in March 2000, 'I will have to go and "beg" for fuel this week as the Provincial Transport Board will not give us any'.

For all criminal justice agencies, the general lack of operational funds limits training, management audits, vehicle and infrastructure maintenance, and limits the mobility to apprehend offenders, take prisoners to courts, supervise community based orders, buy supplies, market produce, conduct prisoner education programs and lobby communities. There are no maintenance regimes for equipment and photocopiers, computers break down frequently or run out of ink cartridges that cost from K120 to K220 each, typewriters run out of ribbons and there is usually a shortage of printer paper. Yet in this environment, police officers are expected to produce court briefs, police prosecutors are expected to present adequately researched prosecution cases to courts, community correctional officers are expected to produce pre-sentence and pre-parole reports, custodial correctional officers are expected to develop prisoner rehabilitation programs and all are expected to keep regular statistics. When such commitments cannot be fulfilled, criminal justice agency staffers suffer enormous loss of face resulting in diminished energy and interest—some become ill or die of stress-related disorders—and productivity is severely reduced. As a consequence, the safety of the public is devalued, and the right of remand prisoners to have a 'fair and public hearing…to determine his rights and obligations…of any criminal charge against him' as soon as possible after their imprisonment, is ignored (*Post-Courier* 10 December 1998:20–1). This reality makes farcical the crime control rhetoric of politicians who spend only one per cent of recurrent budget on law and order.

Village courts—whose officials remain unpaid for long periods of time, but whose services are in greater demand due to worsening social conditions—are often pressured to take more responsibility for offender punishment and rehabilitation by ordering community work instead of fines. For example, in April 2000, it was reported that offenders found guilty by village courts would do community work when local and district courts endorse orders (*Post-Courier* 6 April 2000:3). While this appears conducive to involving communities in crime prevention and control, money to buy stationery to keep records of community work hours, to train court officials and supervisors, to pay court officials and supervisors, to buy tools and other incidentals to perform community work, and above all, to audit activity to maintain accountability and retain community support, is not available. In June 1999, Barakau village court outside Port Moresby, went into recess because village court officials had not been paid. At Baruni in the NCD, court officials say supervisors cannot patrol the village at night and then be expected to supervise community workers by day for the same pay. Village court officials are willing to play a greater part in crime control but the continuous lack of financial resource provision exposes the government's lack of commitment to customary dispute resolution and to community justice. Peace officers and court clerks receive only K22.22 per month, magistrates K26.64 per month, the deputy village court chairman K29.06 per month and the chairman K32.70 per month (*The National* 10 March 2000:Weekender:3). Failure to pay village court officials is illustrated by the example of Woitape, a half-hour flight from Port Moresby, where in May 1997 village court magistrates and peace officers had not been paid for years due to insufficient funds from the Central Province Provincial Government.

Recommendations for policy development have been made in reports on law and order commissioned by several prime ministers since the mid 1970s. The reports reiterate similar themes: better coordination between criminal justice agencies, more community policing, more community-based supervision, the introduction of alternative dispute resolution, the upgrading of information systems, the training of criminal justice personnel, the provision of adequate resources to criminal justice agencies, the provision of adequate education and health services to communities, and provision of improved infrastructure. A major recommendation by the 1984 Clifford Report to the NEC was that a new law and order policy be adopted involving informal institutions in the maintenance of order and providing adequate resource support to institutions (Clifford, Morauta and Stuart 1984a). In 1993, the National Law Order and Justice Council drew up a policy approved by the NEC. The key to policy implementation was six programs: local-level relations and relations with wider social and economic concerns; research and information systems; human and other resource development; coordination efficiency; corruption and management; and law and order sector capacity budgeting and planning. Wider community involvement, mediation and conflict resolution and national awareness campaigns were also included in the policy working parties' program for implementation. A change of government in 1995 resulted in the replacement of the National Law Order and Justice Council by the Law Order and Administration Committee. The new committee was advised of the work of the old committee and given access to its policy documents. It too was charged with producing a law and order policy. No policy was forthcoming. Eventually in 1999, Sinclair Dinnen, a Senior Research Fellow with the Research School of Pacific and Asian Studies at The Australian National University was commissioned by the Morauta Government to develop a law and order policy. Dinnen's belief is that informal methods of crime control offer better and cheaper alternatives to state methods. He also argues that Papua New Guinea's strong sense of community needs to be harnessed because modernised customary laws continue to wield significantly more influence at village level than state controls. The essence of Dinnen's law and order policy, drawn up in cooperation with law and order staff, was a focus on community participation at national, provincial, district and village levels. While the policy was approved, and an awareness tour conducted nationally, the realities of resource deficiencies (which result in poor case clearance rates, court delays, prison overcrowding, few community based orders and intermittent village court sittings) challenge its implementation.

The resounding concern is that issues of politics, leadership, accountability, corruption and state capacity limit the success of both state or community crime control strategies. A lack of political will to turn rhetoric into action and a lack of fiscal discipline to provide resources to meet basic operational demands, undermines agency ability and commitment to work with communities to prevent and control crime. With the exception of pockets of professionalism and an increased awareness of the need to plan, criminal justice agencies lack consistent management strategies that create a sense of ownership of organisational visions, missions and goals that manifest in organised, disciplined frameworks to support sustainable action. While community involvement can indeed strengthen crime control and crime prevention initiatives, and cut costs, essential elements needed for involvement are a change in the perception of criminal justice agency staff of their roles, appropriate legislation to facilitate change, and follow up to ensure that staff are aware of legislation (Chattoraj 1996). While current legislation and policy has been written in Papua New Guinea to facilitate a more rehabilitative approach and to encourage community involvement, uncertainty exists amongst criminal justice agency staff as to whether or not they are law enforcers, reformation officers, or both. While RPNGC and PNGCS recruits are trained in altruistic behaviour, such training is rarely reinforced in the workplace. Correctional officers are often 'self taught' because there is 'no one around to teach us'. The late Benedict Kasi, a senior PNGCS officer, was often vocal in his concerns regarding poor organisational management. On 26 March 1999, he wrote to the Commissioner, that 'delegations require reinforcement and recognition and regular "hands on" monitoring by managers' adding that the lack of leadership manifests in frustration, low morale, poor discipline, corrupt practice, low productivity, deployment deficiencies and workload imbalances (personal communication, Bendict Kasi).

A major challenge for the police service and the correctional service, is to change the perception of their members from that of reactive law enforcers and guards to that of public servants who play a major role in correcting offending behaviour—by putting legislation and policy into practice daily—setting high personal standards of behaviour and working with other agencies and communities to control crime. In the meantime, internal and external power plays that advocate draconian strategies to contain prisoners and control crime may cause extreme damage to effective crime control endeavours. The media reports disgruntled citizens advocating harsh conditions, bread and water diets and chain gangs for prisoners. However, when a very senior correctional officer refers to prisons as 'holiday camps' and suggests that PNGCS must 'guarantee the safety and security' of people, the principles of the new law and order policy are undermined (Sikani 2000:11).

Poor employment conditions within criminal justice agencies govern the level of product output and influence the way practitioners think and behave. Sustainable crime control strategies are very much dependent upon meeting the basic needs of criminal justice agency staff and incarcerated persons. For example, correctional officers believe—with justification—that prisoner escapes are not their fault, but the fault of the government for not providing resources to clear court backlogs, reduce prison overcrowding, improve prisoner accommodation and ensure regular supplies of prisoner rations. A staff member at a provincial prison said, 'If you want prisoner rehabilitation we have to be looked after first. We receive no recognition only criticism, staff housing is rundown, there is no transport for our children to attend school, we wait a long time for leave fares, managers do not tell us what to do and they use government vehicles to conduct private business' (Karella and Whittaker 1998:2). On 4 January 1999, the late Benedict Kasi wrote to the Commissioner alerting him to 'the problems…affecting the Department…[resulting] in the downfall of morale and discipline…'. He said, 'our staff basic needs are not being provided by the state…uniforms, housing, promotion, overtime, etc…[manifesting in] the downfall of…job commitment and dedication' (personal communication, Benedict Kasi). The commanding officer of Bihute prison in the EHP expressed similar sentiments in a brief to headquarters dated 30 March 1999. He said, 'how can we expect personnel to perform to their best…when their quarters are not…maintained…and…expectations [do] not materialise' (Pitts 1999d:9–10).

Impact of Australian aid-funded institutional strengthening projects

There have been high expectations of the Australian aid program by PNG politicians and their delegates to 'fix' problems, provide resources and take the lead in crime prevention strategies. While this view is changing gradually, sentiments continue to be made by PNG academics and politicians that 'advisers cause the problems' and Australian-funded projects often produce 'minimal medium and long-term results' (Hiambohn 2000a:2). One reason for this state of affairs is that Australia's aid program struggles to satisfy a triple mandate comprising foreign policy, commercial benefits to Australia and the reduction of poverty. Its desire to fulfil all agendas at the same time often results in reduced development effectiveness. Aid projects become output—rather than outcome—oriented, losing sight of country and agency priorities and can displace—rather than complement—local initiative. The Australian Government believes that the biggest development challenge facing Papua New Guinea is governance and institutional capacity that manifests in good leadership, integrity and transparency in decision making, prioritisation of public investment and a skilled, efficient and incorruptible public service (AusAID 1997). However, institutional strengthening is a time-consuming business that takes years of concentrated effort, much longer than the life of most aid projects. The process to increase agency capacity must also be intense because organisational culture must change and for this to occur, aid program focus must be on strengthening agency management and financial systems and developing human resources. Institutional strengthening aid to PNG criminal justice agencies does include long-term technical advice on finance and management systems and human resource development, training and infrastructure support. The Australian managing contractor ACIL Australia Pty Ltd delivers the aid to PNG criminal justice agencies through teams of specialist advisers who work with managers, advising on policy, financial and management systems, human resource and infrastructure development. The quality

Table 6 Criminal justice agency absorptive capacity limits to institutional strengthening

Project demands which influence absorptive capacity	Environmental influences to organisational absorptive capacity
Adviser under pressure succumbs to 'doing' role	High recipient agency project expectations
Poor project design	Corruption
AusAID development expectations managing contractor profit-making expectations	Minimal commitment by recipient agency of human and other resources for project
Project team leadership and communication skills may be poor	Adverse social and economic conditions
Excessive adviser's report writing demands which reduce interaction with counterparts and stall project outputs	Minimal time commitment by recipient agency of project priorities on top of daily operational demands
PMRG perceptions and advice to AusAID on project needs may omit underlying limits.	Political influence and interference
	Minimal support by PNG Government
AusAID's excessive accountability demands Project may be output rather than outcome oriented	Poor resource availability of recipient agency to meet daily operational demands
Poor cultural sensitivity and awareness of adviser	Poor counterpart skills, ownership, understanding or commitment
AusAID inflexibility to change milestone components to suit changing needs and demands of recipient agency and local environments	

of aid delivery is monitored by an in-country AusAID representative attached to the Australian High Commission and through an independent team of specialists, called the Project Monitoring and Review Group, contracted by AusAID to visit projects at least bi-annually. Despite this, the impact of institutional strengthening on PNG criminal justice agencies has been minimal. This is due to the inability of agencies to absorb, implement and sustain new philosophies and practices within contractual timeframes. Low absorptive capacity occurs for the reasons already stated, including weak leadership, inadequate administrative systems and human and material resource capacity. Table 6 illustrates the large number of limits.

Conflicts amongst aid players resulting from miscommunication and frustration, and ambitious project-driven initiatives, governed by inflexible budgetary criteria, conflict with operational realities and aid agendas to meet individual deadlines, further reducing absorption of new ideas and practise to enhance capacity. These conflicts are illustrated in Table 7.

To be effective, reform programs need to be tailored to institutional capacity and should focus only on the core functions of government. Ambitious agendas that exceed institutional capacity fail to deliver acceptable outcomes (Fallon and Sugden 1998). The 1997 Committee of Review on AusAID warned against 'strong conditionality' that can militate against local ownership and commitment, and stressed the value of setting limits in relation to how much a donor should impose its preferences (AusAID 1997). There are many willing criminal justice agency staffers, but their desire and capacity to absorb new information and practice is often inhibited by a combination of factors. Resource scarcity within criminal justice agencies for example, overrules development objectives until operational priorities, such as payment of wages, utilities, food bills, vehicle and equipment maintenance, are met. Such scarcity too, means that aid projects working with criminal justice agencies may need to fund postage, paper, computer cartridges and equipment maintenance to meet agreed aid deadlines.

AusAID describes 'sustainability' as continued local action stimulated by a project, services and incentives generated as a result

Table 7 Examples of conflicts in relations between criminal justice agency stakeholders

Relationships	Examples of reasons for conflicts in relationships
Australian community with Australian Government/AusAID	High expectations of aid inputs by Australian public to reduce crime, increased investment and travel opportunities. AusAID commitment to aid expenditure targets, future financial allocations and parliamentary justifications. Australian Government has defence considerations.
AusAID with recipient criminal justice agency	Minimal pragmatic awareness by AusAID to project target delays. Justification of aid expenditure by Australian Government Minister. Recipient agency reluctance to divulge negative information to AusAID that may result in project termination.
AusAID with managing contractor	Minimal pragmatic understanding by AusAID of cultural, political, social and economic inhibitors of project output. Satisfaction by AusAID with project output before payment. Project cash flow problems of managing contractor. AusAID accountability to Australian Government Minister.
Managing contractor with project team	Managing contractor is profit-oriented. Managing contractor can have minimal pragmatic awareness of cultural, political, social and economic inhibitors to project output. AusAID pressure on managing contractor to complete project components within timeframes.
AusAID with project team	AusAID can have minimal pragmatic awareness of obstacles and time involved to achieve project component outputs. Negative PMRG reports due to minimal pragmatic awareness by PMRG of cultural, social and economic inhibitors to component output.
Project team with recipient criminal justice agency	High expectations of recipient agency of project teams to fix systems and fund ventures. Political interference of recipient agency and resultant fear can stall project related action. Lack of ownership of project by agency and consequent minimal commitment to project. Also, agency perceptions of project team 'take over' due to inadequate consultation. Project team members may be

	intolerant, or lack understanding of inhibitors to project outputs. Project members pressured into line management roles.
Project team with Project Monitoring and Review Group	PMRG can lack understanding of the cultural, social, economic and political inhibitors to achieving outputs and criticise team initiatives in reports to AusAID.
Recipient agency with Project Monitoring and Review Group	PMRG may not be sensitive of internal issues and may presume to understand how to accelerate component outputs and 'fix' systems.
Project team with PNG Government	PNG Government may have minimal awareness of project design, constraints on project team and have too higher expectations regarding project team output.
Project team with PNG communities	PNG communities may have minimal awareness of constraints on project team or too higher expectations of what the project can achieve within a particular timeframe.
Recipient criminal justice agency with PNG communities	PNG communities may have minimal awareness of constraints on criminal justice agencies. PNG communities intolerant of corrupt practices of agency.
PNG communities with PNG Government	PNG communities intolerant of corrupt practices and lack of discipline of government politicians and public servants.
Australian Government with PNG Government	Australian Government expects PNG Government to perform and to retain defence and trade relationship. PNG Government expects Australian Government to continue assistance and defence and trade relationships.

of increased local capacity, and project initiated goods and services still delivered and maintained five years after project completion (AusAID 1997). The reality is that unless AusAID makes substantial contributions to project-related running costs over the first five years, projects may flounder. To this end AusAID believes that it may have to finance large proportions of project costs during the investment stage, then subsequent aspects of recipients' asset maintenance and related governance improvement programs (AusAID 1999). AusAID realised the need to meet project running costs in the early stages of the PNGCS project when it commissioned the Bomana prison to manufacture furniture for the new staff training college which was also funded by AusAID. The objective was to provide income to PNGCS and the opportunity for skills development of staff and prisoners. To sustain the project within the resource deficient environment of the PNGCS and to achieve production deadlines, AusAID bought materials and funded joinery running costs, including a workshop machine maintenance regime, and paid PNGCS for the furniture. The project was a success, providing a positive learning environment for joinery staff and prisoners and producing good quality furniture. A drawback of this approach is that project ownership is not transferred to recipients. In this case, the project was known as 'AusAID's project' as the Australian managing contractor and AusAID monitored production closely with selected PNGCS members and met all costs (in this example the stakes were high, for if production deadlines had not been met, AusAID would have been liable for significant contractual penalties).

Despite depleted organisational capacity, some notable industry successes are due to the management and networking ability of certain dedicated PNGCS personnel. For example, in 1998 and 1999, Bomana women prisoners and Kerevat male prisoners produced and harvested rice. Inspired by these successes, the PNGCS Commissioner announced that rice would be grown at major coastal prisons to cut prisoner ration costs (*Post-Courier* 13 July 2001:3). For such projects to succeed, astute planning ability and high quality management is crucial as organisational and environmental conditions tend to constrain consistent production and expansion. For example, human resource availability in prisons is limited by frequent urgent operational demands—prisoner lockups after escapes, poor discipline, delegations, deployment, supervision and routines. As a result, prisoner industry real work time is reduced to four and a half hours a day after roll call (excluding lunch) and up to knockoff. So while the Bomana prison has a vast area of arable land suitable for agricultural development, and the institution appears to have sufficient staff and male prisoners to make and maintain gardens, industry development and sustainability is dependent on better organisation of labour by management, sufficient material resources, and an efficiently administered Prison Industries Trust Account to fund running costs. These requirements are also crucial to offset natural disasters like floods, and cope with the long dry season that can last up to eight months of the year.

In theory, an efficiently-run Prison Industries Trust Account provides a solid financial base for industry sustainability. Prison managers rely on such an account to pay for recurrent industry expenditure, like seed and stock purchases, or tractor and water pump maintenance and repair. While a clear and simple system appeared to be in place to manage the Prison Industries Trust Account and to approve and distribute funds in 1999, it failed. This was because there was little or no management; moreover, the fund was exploited by certain individuals for their own ends. The Prison Industry Trust Account Committee was supposed to meet regularly to approve industry funding. Several commanders waited over a year for responses to funding applications but all attempts failed to convene a committee meeting. When the Committee eventually convened in February 2000, it was discovered that the trust fund had been rorted and there had been little or no action to discipline or suspend those responsible. The fund's credibility was thus damaged, industry initiatives were stalled, and frustrated prison managers established illegal 'slush funds' to cover running costs of the surviving industry.

Such non-transparent regimes can undermine aid effectiveness and, combined with rigid institutional strengthening criteria, can lock advisers on to a contractual treadmill that achieves little within prescribed timeframes. Indeed, achieving 'outcomes' rather than simply 'outputs', requires a degree of donor budget flexibility when working within weak administrative structures, especially when counterparts are either not committed to project aims or are poor managers and there are severe material resource deficiencies. This scenario is particularly pertinent to the Correctional Service Development Project which, although reputed to be 'going well' will be terminated in September 2002. The Office of National Planning stated that 'Australian managing contractors are not working hard enough within the given period' and some projects, especially the

RPNGC and Correctional Service Development Projects, 'are consuming a lot of time and available resources that could be used elsewhere' (Office of National Planning 1999a:6). In reality, most technical advisers work diligently in very difficult administrative and sometimes environmental conditions plagued by equipment breakdowns, materials shortages, counterpart absences and staff deployments, and still manage to work with available staff to initiate policy, develop management regimes and write procedural manuals. Demands on technical advisers emanate from the recipient agency, the Australian managing contractor and AusAID—the latter two requiring monthly reports, quarterly reports, six-monthly reports, annual reports and other reports on demand, while regular monitoring and review teams also require reports. An adviser on an AusAID funded project estimated that she spent almost one-third of her time writing such reports. Recipient agencies have expectations of advisers' performance beyond the scope of their contracts, and in times of crisis, the adviser's role of advising merges with the 'doing' role of line management. For example in 1998, the technical adviser for PNGCS finance and administration acted in a line management role for almost 12 months, due to the non-availability of a counterpart to produce an annual budget, rationalise staff cutbacks and keep the finance section going.

While mistakes are made in project design due to unfamiliarity with agency environments and a lack of appreciation of the impact of resource deficiencies, concerted attempts are also made during the life of projects to work with counterparts to review work plans and rectify mistakes. For action to be sustainable, strategies require the commitment of agency managers, a high degree of accountability, material resource availability, and political will. With a view to providing a 'Best Practice Model' to assist delivery-practitioners to achieve successful institutional strengthening, AusAID commissioned Mark Turner of The University of Canberra to develop a set of criteria. Turner's model specified institutional capacity, mutual understanding of project design, joint implementation, organisational desire to build up management systems, skills and capabilities, interaction ability with key external institutions, and integrated monitoring and evaluation. Yet the model does not fit with the reality of PNG criminal justice agencies or other government agencies which struggle to meet the criteria with only a thin layer of competent officials, antiquated and inefficient systems and a general lack of administrative capacity (AusAID 1997). Internal and external political influences, depleted financial and management systems and poor communication within organisations, or with other agencies, deplete capacity. Staff members are generally undisciplined and both staff and managers are frequently absent without explanation. For example, in late 1998, I worked with a team of PNGCS counterparts to draft a practice and procedure manual for the new minimum security facility at the Bomana prison. Before the manual could be written, training in research and manual collation was needed. It took almost three months and a great deal of lobbying for the team to be released for the task. In early 1998, I worked with counterparts to develop a monthly report-writing proforma pack to simplify reporting for low literacy personnel. Approval to test the pack took six months, it was another month before the pack could be distributed and another three months before it was photocopied and distributed to prisons (the timeframe for project output expired in August 1998). By October 1999, the reporting pack was being used spasmodically. Management meeting postponements and cancellations, staff absences, photocopier breakdowns, insufficient funds to buy stationary and postage stamps, closure of provincial post offices due to robberies, inability of prisons to collect mail due to lack of transport, and inability of prisons to post returns due to absence of funds to buy postage stamps all held up implementation.

The 1997 Report of the Committee of Review on AusAID stated that best donor practice is 'to pursue maximum development effectiveness even when it means implementing important, but low-profile activities…' (AusAID 1997:164). For the PNGCS, however, such low-profile activities as prison industry production and prisoner rehabilitation require human and financial resources, and the utilisation of such resources requires training at all levels together with management leadership ability. Two major challenges for criminal justice agencies are: first, to work within the confines of national and provincial budgets and limited aid assistance, and second, to focus training on legislation, leadership, human resource, asset management and administrative skills, including file access and storage and basic office procedure (Pitts 1999b:7).

Conclusion

Papua New Guinea criminal justice agencies work to contain crime, but political interference, weak leadership, deficient administration systems and endemic corruption often stymie their efforts. In contrast, the PNG crime industry is better led, better organised and has greater human resource availability.

While some criminal justice agency problems have been addressed through policy development and institutional strengthening, many initiatives have stalled due to the indolence of successive governments who are not committed to behavioural or fiscal discipline, transparent decision making or adequate budgetary allocations. Some reforms have been too ambitious for agency absorptive capacity, and while projects like the Correctional Service Development Project are said to be 'going well', project time is very limited, sapped by operational demands or reactions to perceived crises, many of which simply satisfy political agendas.

AusAID-funded institutional strengthening projects can assist criminal justice agencies to maintain infrastructure, develop policies and systems and train staff. Yet advisers cannot do the work and fix the problems. This is the responsibility of the government. When advisers are drawn into line management 'doing' roles to address crises and meet contractual deadlines, less agency development occurs and more conflicts erupt amongst players: reducing aid project effectiveness.

5
Criminal justice agency and community links

In Papua New Guinea there is not just one community, one culture or one language. There are many communities, many cultures and sub-cultures, and over seven hundred languages. Perceptions of crime vary from community to community and are sometimes at odds with state law. Some state controls are not acceptable to communities and some community controls are not acceptable to the State. Crime control methods sanctioned by communities are based upon shared values and opinions. This means that the underlying law based on 'custom' varies from community to community—changing according to need—unlike state law, based on the Westminster model, which is constant.

Leadership integrity and human rights

Article 21 (1) of the Universal Declaration of Human Rights 1948–98 states that everyone has the right to take part in the government of his country, directly or through freely chosen representatives. The

PNG Constitution strengthens this philosophy, declaring that all citizens have the same rights, privileges, obligations and duties irrespective of race, tribe, origin, political opinion, colour, creed, religion or sex. It also gives each citizen the right of free speech and freedom of expression through a free media (*Constitution of the Independent State of Papua New Guinea 1975*:Section 55). Yet when leaders do not uphold the rights, dignity, and safety of citizens—by denying citizens opportunities to participate in decision making, in education of state procedures and processes; do not institute and monitor a Code of Ethics and Practice for politicians and public servants; do not respond positively to citizen protests; and moreover do not commit adequate resources to development initiatives—neither state nor community sanctions can sustain human rights practice that protects and benefits citizens. As a result, citizens suffer the social and economic costs of neglect, and respond with detachment, disinterest, and minimal commitment to state-driven initiatives.

There are several essential elements that can either encourage participation in crime control, or destroy it. They are the quality and morality of leadership, the way leadership manifests in public perception and in public institutions, and the determination of leaders to obtain positive change and greater participation. Leadership is the core of governance. It is impossible for leaders to enforce high standards of integrity in the public service while they tolerate corrupt behaviour in their own ranks. When political leaders are corrupted and fail to demand high standards, the structure of administrative integrity weakens, economic development erodes, human resources are wasted and the national economy crumbles (Mohan 1996). Moreover, the public loses trust in criminal justice agencies and public willingness to participate and cooperate in crime control diminishes. The quality of criminal justice service also diminishes, leaving a disillusioned and apathetic population, unprotected and undeveloped politically, socially and economically (Chan Kin-hung 1996, Grabosky 1996).

Citizens naturally demand higher moral and ethical standards and enhanced vigilance, and deplore the apathy in political ranks towards crime. In Papua New Guinea, however, fraudulent leaders have eroded public institutions, and weak administrators who are politically influenced do not enforce controls or prosecute alleged offenders. The Sandline and Cairns Conservatory political scandals, provincial government corruption probes, losses of K245 million from the National Provident Fund, and government arrears of K65 million to the Public Officers Superannuation Fund, have undermined government and leadership integrity and pushed the economy to the verge of bankruptcy (Nonggorr 1998g, *Post-Courier* 9 March 2000:3, *The National* 14 June 1999:6, Hunt 2000). The fraud in the National Provident Fund and the Public Officers Superannuation Fund may well be the catalyst PNG citizens need to insist on the prosecution and punishment of offenders, but for citizens to make protest and participate in decisions to enforce accountability, they need to know what their constitution says; what their responsibilities are; how the constitution links with other legislation; and how it can be applied to protect their rights. Such public consciousness will assist law enforcement and protect human dignity (Soetjipto 1990). Many PNG citizens do not believe they can make their constitution work for them and express passive 'faith' statements and 'let's hope' words such as: 'he has his own way of doing things', 'he tried his best', 'it will take time', 'I have faith in God' and in emotional speeches about what 'should be done' or a feigning of detachment by 'head-lowering' or silence. These modes of expression are a result of victimisation, disillusionment and fear and a general lack of citizen confidence. Many communities have turned inward, having lost faith in their leaders, in the capacity of their nation state and in their own ability to participate in political decisions, saying, 'whatever we try to do' we are stopped by 'no resources, no government support' or 'politicians who rob us'. In early 2000, one public servant I know grew a beard in mourning for his organisation.

Participants from a variety of countries in a United Nations Asia and Far East Institute workshop called 'Fraud against Enterprises and Consumers', concluded that 'fraud is the most damaging of all crimes' and most societies are ambivalent about it (UN Asia and Far East Institute 1995:237). Yet 'corrupt' conduct by Christian standards is also considered misconduct in Asian religious texts that pre-dated Christianity. Bribery, the worst form of corruption, is called *gin muong* (nation eating) in Thailand, *tan wu* (greedy impunity) in China, *oshoku* (dirty job) in Japan and *pungli* (unofficial levies) in Indonesia (Mohan 1996:74). In Papua New Guinea, deals are done between public servants and others 'in the Melanesian way'; that is through giving and receiving gifts for favours. One public servant told me, 'I give him a bit and he gives me a bit...but it's not a bribe'. When I asked how 'gift giving' fitted in with the 'human rights' elements of the constitution, I was informed 'it didn't' because 'human rights' in Papua New Guinea are different from 'human rights' in Australia and 'we Papua New Guineans haven't caught up yet'. Several PNG writers: John Nonggorr, Peter Donigi, Sir Anthony Siaguru and Mavara Ao Sere believe 'traditional codes of honour' have been lost, and unless the legal system can monitor and control public and private sectors properly, 'we are merely scratching around the surface of the problem' (Sere 1996:143).

Community participation in crime prevention

Inviting communities to participate in crime control without prosecuting and punishing fraudulent leaders is a devious act in itself. It is a device to divert citizenry focus and energy from core issues and at the same time, assures their failure by giving them no long-term financial or extension support in the form of basic and specific goods and services to sustain crime control initiatives. Nevertheless, there are some diligent individuals in criminal justice agencies, community and donor organisations who battle resource-deficiencies to prevent and control crime. Church-based community organisations run prisoner development programs, juvenile detention centres, prisoner halfway houses, prisoner after-care programs and vocational schools, and support women and youth. Some businesses employ released prisoners, others fund accommodation for young homeless people or assist criminal justice agencies with resources and business development advice. Most community agencies say they want to be asked for input by state agencies. For example, at a community forum at Boram prison in Wewak in June 1999, community members said they 'did not know' of the efforts of PNGCS to rehabilitate prisoners and 'wanted to be asked' to help. The result of the forum was that a church group proposed a prisoner after-care program 'if funding could be secured'. Many links are already established between criminal justice agencies and community organisations and much offer valuable support to state agencies when government subsidies and other resources are available. Subsidies are rarely paid however and programs often flounder. In early 1999, neither the Catholic-run Hohola juvenile detention centre nor the Salvation Army-run Badili juvenile detention centre had received government subsidies in several years. The Hohola centre had no residents and the Badili centre survived on charity to feed and clothe 19 boys between the ages of 13 and 17 years and to provide a rudimentary literacy program.

In 1989, PNGCS initiated a community outreach program called the Inmate-Outmate Program. The purpose of the program was to provide awareness to schools and communities on criminality, prison life and prisoner needs. It proved popular and generated much community support and interest but ceased due to resource difficulties in the mid 1990's. The program was reintroduced before a village court session at Baruni village in the NCD in June 1998—a team of 10 male and female correctional officers and male and female prisoners from Bomana prison conducting an awareness session. Even though the team was late arriving because their old vehicle had a flat tyre on the way, over 250 residents waited, and then responded very positively—later inviting the team to return. Other village court magistrates from Hanuabada, Tatana and Pari expressed interest in the program. The next month, the Motu–Koitabu Local Level Government Council—the governing body of NCD Motu-Koitabu villages—promised invitations. Events prevented this however, the Motu–Koitabu Council chairman was sacked, councillors became pre-occupied in political manoeuvring for leadership, and the PNGCS vehicle, used to transport prisoners and staff to re-introduce the program at Baruni, broke down completely. A year later when a new prison vehicle was procured, it was not made available for the program, and prison management was diverted to operational demands like prison overcrowding, escapes, ration scarcity, shortages of electricity and water (due to non-payment of accounts), and deficiencies in human resources. The demands of a new AusAID-funded infrastructure project, a drought, a flood and equipment breakdowns, also inhibited community outreach.

In 1992, the Foundation for Law, Order and Justice and the RPNGC conducted a workshop on crime prevention and community policing. The criminal justice system and social policy agencies were represented. Workshop consensus was that there should be a move away from reactive policing to community-based crime prevention. This strategy was to be supported by a community policing policy to channel scarce resources into development activities at community level and to perform a crime prevention role. Thus freeing up criminal justice agencies to concentrate on more serious offences (Egan 1992).

Police initiatives in the 1990s to increase community participation also included the establishment of Police Community Consultative Committees in provincial centres. These committees form a central part of the strategy of the RPNGC Community Policing Directorate 'to involve the community with policing in securing a safer community' and recognising that community awareness influences police goals of preserving law and order, enhances leadership and accountability and improves infrastructure and financial management (RPNGC 1998:DA3). Other community policing strategies implemented include a reserve constabulary or auxiliary police support to regular police. In addition sport, recreational and cultural events, literacy, religious fundraising, self-help and beautification programs, youth liaison and rehabilitation targeting ex-criminals, community awareness programs, neighbourhood watch and schools programs, housing police and their families in urban and rural communities, and regular foot patrols were also envisaged. All strategies needed time and money and depended heavily upon material support, human resource deployment, and the commitment and interest of senior police officers, provincial governments and the general community. As a result, some were implemented, some not, and others were short-lived. The broad aim of the Madang Police Community Consultative Commitee was 'to enhance safety and security through community partnerships with police' by informing police of community concerns in relation to crime, advising police how to deal with certain crime, and how to involve communities. At their January 1997 meeting, the committee was keen to enhance communication and initiate practical 'character building' activities to deter youth from crime and keep them 'busy and wholesome'. On 16 January 1997, the Provincial Police Commander and Chairman of the Police Community Consultative Committee, H.R. Kalasim, wrote to the Madang Provincial Government seeking K9,020 to establish rugby and volleyball leagues for youth. On 24 January 1997, the Provincial Office of Social Development wrote back saying they were 'unable to assist' as there had been no budget allocation from the National Government for 'Provincial Youth, Women and Sports Council and Law and Order Activities' for the 1997 financial year, and that the Office had been downgraded to an 'advisory role' (personal communication, Kalasim 1997). Three years later, the MP for Raikos near Madang, Stahl Musa, said that maintaining 'police and community relationships' makes police work 'much easier' and the 'Madang Provincial Government would assist in whatever way possible' (personal communication, Kalasim 1997). Their contribution by January 2000 was, however, two police vehicles and firearms, and a piece of land to build new police staff housing (*Post-Courier* 24 January 2000:3).

'Community-based crime prevention' is often promoted as the most cost effective, long-term solution to preventing and controlling crime. State crime control agencies make efforts to work with communities to develop crime prevention strategies and some communities express their desire to work with state agencies to prevent crime. East New Britain Governor, Francis Koimanrea, said that law and order is maintained when the community bears responsibility for it—discouraging anti-social behaviour by reporting offences, identifying offenders and assisting in their successful prosecution, as 'was the case in…traditional PNG societies' (Koimanrea 1998:2–4). Most 'community based' efforts dissipate when they are caught in the disillusioning and insidious vacuum of political, legal and resource deficiencies. When citizens report offences by prominent people and prosecutions do not eventuate, faith is lost in the criminal justice system to apprehend, prosecute and punish. When political rhetoric does not manifest in resource support, interest is lost in maintaining either order or responsibility. Resource inadequacy crippled community policing in 1998—only 29 police reservists of the 1,000 recruited were trained in NCD in that year and patrolling occurred only 'when resources permitted' (PNG Law and Order Baseline Survey 1996:21–2, Royal Papua New Guinea Constabulary Development Project 1998).

The RPNGC made certain assumptions when initiating community policing. These were: that Police Community Consultative Committees 'can be used to reinforce existing programs' and develop new ones, that the majority of police personnel 'are committed to community policing', that the media 'can be used to spread the word', and that churches and NGOs are 'all working in the same direction' (RPNGC 1999:DA5). Group interest is always in a state of flux given that individuals fill different roles from time to time—their interest groups changing with their roles, their preferences socially influenced and not always consistent (Tisdell 1996). In the diverse socio-economic environment of Papua New Guinea, it is dangerous to assume that groups are committed, will reinforce programs and are all working in the same direction. This is because alliances change rapidly, underlying grievances manifest in inappropriate ways, and resource-deplete communities and local authorities, tired of government rhetoric and promises, 'do nothing' until promises materialise or conflicts are resolved. Police assumptions that 'the majority of staff is committed to community policing', overlooked several obstacles. First, RPNGC and PNGCS personnel will not do 'extra work' unless certain employment conditions are met, and foot patrols are not rated highly by regular police. Second, cultural and social perspectives of police by the public, and the public by police, affect crime control—also influenced positively or negatively by politicians and local leaders. Third, poor human resource management and resource availability threaten initiatives. While legislation offers the police opportunities to practice altruistic values, reinforcement of such values is dependent upon the commitment, interest and autonomy of senior officers. Overcoming strained relationships between police and communities would be cost-effective in the long term, but it is critical that personnel have operating funds, equipment, management support and training (RPNGC 1997). Community outreach also requires realistic plans, enormous commitment and interest. Practitioners must overcome the ingrained attitude that communities are uncooperative, be aware that most communities have no faith in the police, and must realise that efforts for closer communication and cooperation will make small inroads over a long period of time.

Juggling different perspectives to forge closer links between state agencies and communities is challenging. For example, a community work program for prisoners was initiated in 1999. The assumption was that the program could be introduced easily as a cost-effective strategy to provide trusted prisoners with meaningful activity and encourage community participation. While some prison commanders already utilised and welcomed the strategy, others said it was disruptive—their belief being that prisoners working outside prisons would be victimised by those who could not. Some prisoners believed community work was slave labour and 'does not teach us anything', and others did not wish to be seen in prison uniforms. Some communities feared prisoners would commit crimes while outside prisons, but others welcomed and encouraged the strategy and some prisoner work programs had won strong community support. For example in 1999, Kerevat prison conducted a successful prisoner work program sponsored by the Tomar/Vunadidir Local Level Government to build school classrooms. Trusted prisoners delivered agricultural produce to local food retailers, made school desks, and painted signs and pictures for the Kokopo Town Council, businesses and the PNG Tourist Promotion Authority (Pitts 1999f). While communities are discerning in relation to the kind of prisoner rehabilitation they want, extra efforts of prison managers to keep citizens informed can gain more positive responses. Most citizens want to know 'what they can do' to help and are open to reporting crime, learning about the legislation that governs criminal justice practice, and assisting in offender rehabilitation (Pitts 1999g).

A 1998 report on the status of nine correctional institutions recommended several strategies to promote community support. These included: sending PNGCS newsletters and annual reports to governors, provincial government delegates and the judiciary; establishing a prison and community management team to assist prison commanders develop industries and programs; submitting annual plans and funding applications to provincial governments; and increasing liaison with police, courts and parole boards in relation to prison conditions and programs (Karella and Whittaker 1998). In 1998 and 1999 some commanding officers and their staff showed great enthusiasm in working with local communities. Some were guest speakers at schools, women's, youth and other community groups, or attended local law and order meetings. Others worked with community leaders, initiating community work programs, prisoner after-care programs and job placements for released prisoners, while donor agencies like the European Union (EU), Japan International Cooperation Agency (JICA) and business and church based organisations provided industry and life skills training to staff and prisoners. While staff remained enthusiastic, initiatives were spasmodic—all hampered by resource deficiencies.

Community-based sentencing options

The confidence of the National Courts in front-end, community-based sentencing options is undermined by poor village court and community corrections performance. This is caused by resource deficiency and the fact that neither village courts nor community corrections have a sound legislative base with clear procedural manuals outlining operational policy. While international experience indicates that community based supervision is the most successful solution for offender punishment and rehabilitation, it has also shown that the system needs high standards of operation, supervision and reporting to retain community confidence (LISP 1997a). In Papua New Guinea, administrative systems for community-based controls are weak and under-funded. Most village court officials and community correctional officers provide their own stationery, petrol and vehicles, struggle with complex or no reference manuals, and receive little or no monitoring or training. The AusAID-funded Legal Institutional Strengthening Project (LISP) working with A-GD, has made the support and expansion of community-based controls an urgent priority (LISP 1998). While the project prognosis is positive, the downside risks identified are inadequate government funding, protracted timeframes for legislation approval, devolution of authority to provincial governments, problematic retention of unreliable senior A-GD personnel throughout the life of the project, the intervention of political and public opinion regarding punishments, and the need for support of other criminal justice agencies.

For LISP project sustainability and absorption of new initiatives to occur, the PNG Government's appropriation will need to increase (LISP 1997). In 1996, K4 million was deducted from the A-GD Budget for 'transfer' to provinces to pay allowances and other administrative costs of village court officials. No direct payment of allowances however was 'visible' in grants to provinces. Some provincial governments paid partial allowances in arrears but there was no money for supervisory visits or training—and because Village Court Secretariat officials could not travel, standards fell and misinterpretation of functions occurred such as the 'solving' of rape cases (LISP 1997a). Community based supervision of offenders could not be sustained either, and it was thus recommended that community corrections amalgamate with PNGCS (Borrey and Sabadi 1996). While such an amalgamation may provide a flow-on effect to assist offenders to re-integrate into communities, the reality is that PNGCS has barely enough money to feed prisoners and maintain logistical support, let alone administer a community correctional structure. A verbal brief by the PNGCS Commissioner to the Minister in August 1998 emphasised these concerns. The brief suggested strongly that before a decision was made, a working party be convened to consider the level of PNGCS financial allocations in relation to commitments, the level of provincial government support, the availability of persons to rewrite legislation to accommodate the transfer, the cost of the transfer, and related extra training (PNGCS 1998c). Of particular concern was the capacity of PNGCS because in 1998 there was only K731,000 available to draw down each month for operational expenses for 19 prisons, while A-GD had only K900,000 to maintain its community justice programs (PNGCS 1998c). In 1999 and 2000, both PNGCS and A-GD Budgets remained inadequate.

Village courts as community regulators

Resolution of petty crime through the village court system is a popular and well-used option in Papua New Guinea. There are over 1,000 village courts in the country—most functioning at a very basic level, limited by a lack of financial resources, others having been in recess for lengthy periods. While is it recognised that an efficient village court system provides cost-effective community based crime control, realistic and consistent financial support is not forthcoming. Public confidence in their effectiveness wanes as their output diminishes and increases demand for more punitive sentences and inappropriate means of protection (Borrey and Sabadi 1996, LISP 1997, Ahai 2000, *Post-Courier* 25 April 2000:1, 26 April 2000:1).

Regardless of resource limitations, village court officials are still expected to maintain peace and harmony in their localities by mediating and making just and amicable dispute settlements and exercising sentencing in accordance with the principles of natural justice (*Village Court Act 1989:* Section 52, *Constitution of the Independent State of Papua New Guinea*: Section 37). Many village court officials still do. Understandably however, they experience problems in relation to their perceived roles as 'keeper of traditional customs' and at the same time, presider over quasi-Western courts.

The Baruni Village Court in the National Capital District is set up under a tree or in a rundown building and laid out in a similar way to a Western magistrate's court. Village court magistrates, and the clerk who records cases and outcomes, sit behind a rectangular table covered with a white tablecloth decorated with flowers and a sign stating 'Village Court'. A PNG flag is either attached to the wall at the back of the table—if there is a wall—or suspended from the front of the table facing the defendants and the public. Defendants wait their turn with village peace officers. As they are called they go to sit on a bench in front of the magistrates with the complainant. A peace officer sits between them. If there is more than one defendant they may sit on the bench, with a peace officer, facing the magistrates while the complainant sits on another bench at right angles. The public sits or stands behind and around the 'court'. Strict procedure and ritual is followed as in an ordinary magistrates court, with all standing when the magistrates arrive and leave, and bowing to magistrates on entering or leaving the arena. Between May and August 1998, village court cases included alleged stealing, assault and sorcery—for which fines, compensation, good behaviour bonds or combinations of all these penalties were handed down. Magistrates did not sentence offenders to community work because peace officers who would supervise the work are 'up all night anyway'—trying to stop drunken youths from smashing bottles on the road, holding up motorists or damaging property, and peace officers are not paid enough to do two jobs.

On 2 June 1998, the main case for the day at the Baruni Village Court was alleged sorcery, believed to have caused the death of a woman. The complainant, the woman's husband, was from Baruni; the defendant, the woman's lover, lived at Kila Kila. In view of the potentially volatile outcome of sorcery claims, magistrates from both the Motu-Koita villages of Pari and Kila Kila were invited to conjointly consider the allegations. Eight peace officers attended, and villagers of both genders and all ages came to view proceedings. (Magistrates from other villages are typically asked to attend if the defendant, complainant or victim is from another village or there is a need to diminish perceptions of bias relating to sentencing decisions.) Before the court opened, the late Benedict Kasi, the then Bomana Prison Commanding Officer, led an information session for village court magistrates and residents. He said of 655 inmates at Bomana at that time, seven had come through the village court system. He advised magistrates against sentencing offenders to prison for minor offences because 'they will learn to become better criminals'. Mr Kasi emphasised that well resourced, well structured and supervised community work programs are a better option for petty offenders because families of prisoners suffer much hardship due to loss of income and 'if a man goes to jail for one year you can be sure he will go back again for several more'. He sought support for trusted prisoners to attend church outside prison on Sundays and offered the Inmate–Outmate Program to Baruni. The program was conducted the following month.

The sorcery case began. The defendant sat on one side of a peace officer, and the complainant sat on the other. All sat on a bench facing the magistrates. The Pari magistrate leading the session read out the circumstances of the alleged crime. The wife of the complainant died on 14 February 1998. The complainant alleged that before his wife died, the defendant had given her a betel nut with poisoned skin. The complainant told the court his wife had told him she had had a dream in which she saw the defendant obtain poison from a Koirari[1] man at Fourteen Mile. The magistrate said one 'can never believe in dreams as they may or may not be true'. Another magistrate supported him saying 'it was only a dream' and there is no firm evidence that it really happened. It emerged that the defendant and the deceased had had a long love relationship. The defendant told the court he had brought the deceased orange juice from the store before she died. The Pari village court magistrate asked whether or not the juice packet was open. The defendant said it was sealed when he gave it to her. There was prolonged questioning of both the complainant and defendant by magistrates, followed by hushed deliberation on whether or not a genuine act of sorcery had occurred or whether or not the objective of the complainant was to obtain revenge and compensation. In handing down a decision, the Pari magistrate said the court must have proof of the offence but there was none. He summed up by saying, 'we can use custom when it is appropriate, but we must also take note of Western means of proof, for example past experiences, and the court can only make a decision according to the law'. The case was dismissed.

At Woitape in Central Province, sorcery is strongly believed and practised, as it is in many parts of Papua New Guinea. The former Chairman of the Woitape Local Level Government Council, Augustine Mac, believes awareness education about sorcery and illness prevention would be advantageous, and the payment and training of village court officials—who had not been paid for years—would reinforce such education. Woitape village courts are held on demand. Some sentences are biased and discriminatory, and mediation is the favoured form of dispute settlement. For example, there was a case of garden damage caused by a cow belonging to the Catholic Church. It was the fourth time the cow had entered the garden and destroyed crops. The angry garden owner stabbed the cow with a knife wounding it badly. After the third invasion by the cow, the garden owner was given posts and wire to build a fence. He failed to do so. To resolve the dispute, Mr Mac called together village court magistrates and aggrieved parties and sought valuations of the cow and garden. As the value of damage was excessive, aggrieved parties awaited the arrival of the police to deal with the matter that would then go to the village court. The chairman's idea was that compensation and community work be ordered. If the value of damage had not been excessive, the matter could have been settled out of court through mediation, a process for which there is no fixed rule. A way to resolve the cow and garden dispute may have been for the cow and garden owners to come to an agreement on compensation. If they did not agree they could have discussed it with village court magistrates and clan chiefs. If an agreement was still not reached, the chief or chiefs could have made the ultimate decision. This type of decision making is common where there are hereditary chiefs for example, in the coastal village of Kivori Poe, over the range from Woitape.

Augustine Mac and the Chief of all Chiefs of Kivori Poe, Naimo Ikupu, believe village courts can be useful in bridging the gap between the state and community crime control sectors because community morality is reinforced. They also provide a forum to express grievances (Goddard 1992a). Yet the expectations of village courts are far too high in relation to what magistrates can achieve without resources. For village courts to function at their expected level, court officials must be paid, trained and monitored to ensure cases are heard and decisions are fair. Chief Ikupu suggested that for community commitment to development to occur—including the proper function of the village court, community work, and agricultural initiatives—chiefs should be included in local level government decision making for budgetary distribution. On 14 October 1998, at a PNGCS commanding officers' conference, the Assistant Commissioner of the Department of Provincial Affairs, Mr Kila Wari said, 'we are supposed to be deliverers of services down to the rural people' but the coordination and service provision of provincial project planning sub-committees 'is, to put it mildly, very, very bad...there is little commitment by members and an attitude of give us money first before we can do something'. A June 1996 Constitutional Review

Commission report on the restructured system of provincial and local level governments noted the despair of local-level government in not being able to carry out duties. The report stated that while 'the vision and intention of the reform law was to bring services and development to the rural majority...the National Government has not responded positively and accurately to the intent and spirit...[of] the new Organic Law' and this suggests a need for 'a complete review of the country's financial management system and how funds should be diverted to local level governments' (Constitutional Review Commission 1996:5–7). The report also asserted that the Constitutional Review Commission 'has been severely handicapped by the limited funds given to it' and that 'on numerous occasions staff had to forego salaries simply to cover the operational costs necessary to meet deadlines given by the Government' (Constitutional Review Commission 1996:5–7). If village courts are to be a bridging mechanism, they need to attract quality personnel, and recognition must include adequate payment for services, salaries and stipends. Remuneration problems were raised repeatedly by the Village Court Secretariat and magistrates throughout the 1980s but were largely ignored. It is important to move away from the idea that village court officials perform *ex gratia* community services with minimal or no remuneration and to realise that they do need such recognition to help them maintain their autonomy, and to minimise their susceptibility to the control and influence of corrupt personalities. If the state devalues their services by little or no recompense, they cannot be held accountable (Aleck 1992).

The work of village court magistrates is diverse, encompassing both civil and criminal jurisdictions, and requiring skill to prevent crimes from reoccurring. Village court magistrates devote a great deal of time and effort to their work (Jessep 1991, Goddard 1996). Some are also church leaders, working seven days a week, mediating 'family disputes' inside and outside 'court'. The combination of magistrate and church leader is not unusual. Often too, village court magistrates come from powerful traditional family lines, for example, hereditary chieftainships. Some are 'powerful sorcerers' and they can, at the same time, be local level government councillors. It is common for village court magistrates and church elders who have such power bases to be asked to arbitrate disputes between perpetrators and victims outside 'court'. This kind of arbitration may however, amount to a cover up to save the 'face' of the perpetrator and the perpetrator's family. Some cases that fall outside the jurisdiction of village courts are covered up in this way, resulting in compensation by mutual agreement between the families of perpetrators and families of victims. One such case related to an alleged rape and another to alleged incest between father and daughter. In both cases no complaints were made to the police. The alleged rape was settled out of court with the help of village court magistrates and monetary compensation of K5,000 paid by the perpetrator's family to the victim's family. In relation to the incest case, the wife of the perpetrator asked the village court magistrate who was also a church elder, to counsel her husband 'to save face and keep the family together'. In this case, social and economic interaction in the village was such that the 'face' of many families was saved by the magistrate's intervention. In neither case was the female victim compensated for pain and suffering—instead their rights as victims were ignored.

'Custom' that is, the 'usual way of behaving or acting' or in colonial terms, a range of indigenous social behaviour at variance with Anglo-Australian norms (like sorcery, tribal fighting, sexual offences and revenge), did not accommodate the individual rights of victims (Fowler and Fowler 1976, Goddard 1996). The definition of 'custom' remains a problem in terms of legislation and it is difficult for village courts to uphold 'custom' because several different customs may apply in the same sitting when complainants and defendants are from different communities. When disputes occur amongst members of the same community, customary law is 'personalised' and the mediators, who are usually village court officials living in that community, know a great deal about the dispute and are mainly concerned with how to resolve the matter quickly to avoid further internal conflict (Goddard 1992a). In family disputes involving women, the quality of justice and in whose favour it may be obtained, is questioned. Papua New Guinea 'custom' often discriminates against women, contradicting the principles of 'natural justice' enshrined in the Constitution. Village court magistrates have 'a less-than-supportive attitude' towards advancing the equality of women, and the village court system has developed into an effective means of keeping women in subordinate roles (Goddard 1996, Aleck 1992, Law Reform Commission 1987). In several cases between 1989 and 1991, village courts sentenced women to imprisonment for adultery when their husbands had left them alone for several years, or for leaving marriages, or for appearing to consort with other men. No men were sentenced to imprisonment for similar misdemeanours.

Many PNG women say that after marriage, their men generally believe their right to socialise is not affected, yet the privilege does not extend to them and they may be castigated for it. It is also accepted that men control women within marriage, such control sometimes manifesting in the brutality and deprivation of the wife and children. Some village courts formalise this control by sending women to jail for reacting to such behaviour in ways inappropriate to local social mores and in so doing, condone violence perpetrated on women and deny women their rights. Such sentencing contradicts Section 55 of the PNG Constitution that provides equality to all PNG citizens (Gustafsson 1999, Hukula 1986, Jessep 1991). While higher courts have overturned these sentences, the prevailing attitude towards women is disconcerting, especially when the *Customs Recognition Act* (c19) states 'custom will not be recognised or enforced where injustice would result…'. Mary Kamang, president of the Madang Catholic Women's Association and adviser to the Provincial Council of Women, confirms the existence of this attitude. She said, '…our customs and traditions…are preventing [women] from enjoying their human rights'. Each Thursday Madang women wear black to mourn and protest violence against women (Baiom 2000:23). In both the rape and incest cases already mentioned, the victims were told to 'say nothing' or risk being ostracised. A Port Moresby prostitute told me she ran away from home when she was 13, after years of abuse by her uncle. When she told her parents of the abuse, she was beaten by her father and told to 'say nothing' by her mother.

The unofficial work of village court magistrates is sometimes rewarded by gifts of food and beer, but not to the extent to be a systematic alternative to an appropriate wage (Goddard 1996). Some political leaders 'pay' village court magistrates in cash, kind and favours to 'keep things quiet' and at 'village level'. This may occur to avoid publicity of their involvement or the involvement of their relatives in unreported crimes like rape, incest, assault, murder and fraud. 'Arbitrating' magistrates stand to gain kudos for their efforts and are able to maintain strong local power bases. They may believe they 'deserve' some 'traditional' payment to maintain peace and harmony in the community, offsetting poor pay or no pay from the state. Such payments seem warranted when magistrates do not have younger, lucrative wage earners in their families to support them as they are expected to contribute to funerals, bride prices and compensations and to provide for their extended families. In their roles as leaders, they may also be expected to give financial support to political allies. When village court officials are compromised and corrupt or biased practice results, the capacity of both state and community crime controls is reduced to protect citizen rights, maintain community power and absorb positive change—when communities participate in, and condone such practice, they reinforce their own disempowerment and poverty.

Conclusion

Linking crime control methods sanctioned by the state and communities would seem to be the ideal cost-effective solution in a resource deficient environment. but there is little or no contribution from the government. Consequently, non-government agency functions are weakened unless running costs are donor funded. To be effective, the partners in crime control—state and community agencies—need to agree on what actions constitute crime, their level of seriousness within legislative boundaries governing state law, and how crimes will be dealt with. Moreover, communities need to be informed of what the PNG Constitution and other relevant legislation states, and how it is applied. The absorptive capacity of governments and communities needs also to be assessed to ensure strategies are achievable within particular environments. These basic steps require government lead, and need money, human resources and materials that are presently unavailable to the government.

Papua New Guinea citizens express feelings of marginalisation frequently. Most citizens appear to be worn down and wary of false promises and corrupt practices of leaders, and are suspicious of state-driven initiatives. Most would like to act against corrupt practice but fear retribution. Others ignore it and take what they believe is their resource share. The bravest citizens attempt behavioural regulation but can suffer mugging, rape or murder for their trouble. Most citizens perpetuate their own victimisation through inaction, quiescence and misplaced faith in leaders who are undisciplined and neglect constituents—keeping them uninformed, under-resourced and powerless. Citizen involvement in government decision making and action to control crime is often piecemeal. There are insufficient resources to follow through some very worthwhile community-based initiatives to rehabilitate offenders, develop communities and increase income-earning opportunities.

While village courts are a cost-effective and valuable bridging mechanism between formal and informal crime control sectors, and a valuable educative tool for communities on laws, the government does not support them in practice. Provincial and local level governments receive reduced funding allocations that are usually late, while administrative systems at all levels are rarely audited, encouraging misappropriation. When systems are audited, recommendations for action are rarely followed through. A result is that ethical and legislative boundaries are broken down by corruption and cronyism that masquerades as the 'traditional' social mores of sharing and gift giving but which enables some individuals to maintain social prestige, power and wealth at the expense of others. These acts detach communities further from the state and result in sabotage of state-driven initiatives through aggressive acts, inaction or a mirroring of the behaviour of aberrant leaders to obtain a greater share of resources.

Note

1 Koirari people live on the Sogeri plateau in the hills behind Port Moresby.

6
Capacity for crime prevention

Leadership is a vital component of capacity. Communities look to their leaders to provide vision and sustenance and to set standards and lead action to prevent crime to enhance their quality of life. When leadership is not forthcoming—replaced by abuse of power and illicit procurement of wealth—communities suffer resource deficiencies and other neglect, and some citizens mirror the attitudes and behaviour of their leaders. Neither state nor community crime control mechanisms can function independently. Village courts, for example, are designed to arbitrate conflicts according to shared community values and opinions, but they are dependent upon the government for training, remuneration and other resources, which are often rarely forthcoming and meagre. Depleted of resources and unable to meet international, national and sometimes local expectations, court officials are drawn into cycles of political interference and illicit material gain to retain status, recognition and sustenance.

Crime control is often driven by political agendas rather than strategic plans, manifesting in brutal, short-term solutions like raids and curfews that alienate rather than include communities. Efforts to keep the peace beyond the capacity of criminal justice agencies have resulted in the initiation of community controls like vigilante groups and security companies that protect the affluent. A number of security companies are owned by police officers. In 1985, I sold my ten-seater van to a practising commissioned police officer who was starting-up a security company. He wanted the van to 'cart the guards around'. He has since left the police force and become a very rich man. Such ownership of security companies by practising police officers is an obvious conflict of interest—while the RPNGC's mission is to protect the public by reducing crime, profit-oriented security companies are reliant upon a buoyant crime industry. In Port Moresby, for example, where half of Papua New Guinea's security companies operate, competition is fierce and some security bosses retain valuable contracts by 'doing deals' with practising criminals. These 'deals' may include certain strategies to avoid prosecution in relation to alleged offences or to deter targeted break-ins on properties 'guarded' by their companies.

Economic participation, donor dependency and jealousy

Beyond village courts, vigilante groups and security companies, there are a large number of individuals, churches and communities trying to minimise youth and juvenile criminality in a number of ways. All suffer resource deficiencies and all look to the government for vision, guidance and material support, but most survive only because of donor support. Initiatives include micro-enterprise schemes for women, church-run vocational schools, halfway houses for released prisoners, hostels for homeless youth and refuges for battered women and prostitutes, cash cropping, eco-tourism, sports, conflict resolution and mediation programs, and religious advocacy. In early 2000, a Seventh Day Adventist seminarian from Woitape wrote to me. He sought assistance to buy jerseys for five local rugby league teams who participate in 'social matches' and to invite the PNG Rugby

League National Training Coordinator to view end of year games. In March 1998 I had watched players at Woitape, who had walked for two hours over the mountains, play barefoot using coloured devices (rather than jerseys) to differentiate teams. Players and supporters were serious about their sport and sustaining the social games seemed to be an inexpensive way to focus and occupy youth, keep them fit and enhance skills like team work, fair play and leadership.

On several occasions during my work with PNGCS I was asked to advise on proposals aimed at involving youth in legitimate activity to deter them from crime. Proposals included the establishment of released prisoner halfway houses and community-based enterprises in Port Moresby and surrounding districts involving the harnessing of natural resources and the marketing of produce. Small business is the most popular venture in both urban and rural environments and the subject of many proposals to government departments or donors. One proposal sought K50,000 to start up a youth training centre to assist released prisoners through training and counselling to secure employment or start a small business (Ove 1999:6). Another proposed an entrepreneurial skills training program for prisoners at a cost of K2,000 for a two-day course. Both proposals targeted the Correctional Service Development Program for funding rather than PNGCS. This was because, as indicated in the entrepreneurial skills proposal, there are 'shortfalls in government funding' (Mato Business and Development Consultancy 1999:1). In 1998, I spoke with several prisoners and their families who wished to start up small business schemes to occupy deviant youth. On 5 May 1998, a prisoner, whom I shall call Joseph wrote

> I have been a gang leader and led a gangster's life since the 1980s but have realised now the need to live a normal way of life [and] in 1997 [I joined] the prison church fellowship [and am now] an elder of our Seventh Day Adventist group. My ambition is to discourage and deter youth from NCD and Central Province from making the same mistakes as I have by involving them in activities and organising fellowship groups as I have a reputation and large influence over youths in my area.

Joseph's idea was to give urban-born Port Moresby youth an

opportunity to experience rural life by working on agricultural projects at Cape Rodney 200 kilometres east of Port Moresby. He needed Department of Agriculture and Livestock (DAL) assistance to achieve this. In another case, a prisoner whom I shall call Paul wrote to me on 21 August 1998 seeking advice on agricultural project expansion at a village near Bereina 60 miles west of Port Moresby. Paul was educated to Grade 12 and had completed several management courses. He was serving a 12-month sentence for possession of marijuana. His proposal was well-presented and he was aware of the market value of agricultural produce. He offered as part of collateral for a loan, communally-owned land and a 30-seater PMV, but his production costs were underestimated. I was also privy to a Goilala district business plan which proposed youth development through road cleaning and building contracts, cash cropping vegetables and farming cattle, poultry and sheep. The Goilala is a very poor district and the purpose of the plan was to deter unemployed youth from 'walking over the hills' to join criminal gangs in Port Moresby. I passed Joseph's and Paul's proposals to DAL and contacted the Small Business Development Corporation (SBDC) who said they would visit Joseph and Paul in prison and recommended a similar course of action for the Goilala proposal. The Director of DAL's Export Crops Promotion and Development Program wrote back that while the division could assist with 'technical investigation and assessment' in collaboration with provincial DALs, the division 'is at the moment financially handicapped to travel to the concerned community area to assist…'. The Director recommended loans be sought through the Smallholder Agriculture Credit Scheme of the Rural Development Bank (RDB) as the purpose of the scheme was to ensure adequate and timely delivery of credit to smallholders, link investments with planned priorities and boost agricultural production, employment and income. I approached the Senior Loans Officer of the RDB who said the bank would consider applications for assistance on their behalf from DAL. At that time DAL, the SBDC and the RDB all suffered severe resource deficiencies and the SBDC and the RDB experienced threats of abolition by the Skate Government. Consequently, in the struggle for institutions to survive neither proposal referred to was followed up.

These proposals contained common restraints to development and goals. The common goals were the minimisation of criminality and improved lifestyles. The common restraints were lack of material or extension support from the Central Province Provincial Government and poor roads. While some sections of the Bereina road have been upgraded, the Cape Rodney road remains very poor—vehicles taking up to eight hours to travel to Port Moresby with people and produce. The Goilala road link is the worst, most vehicles carry two spare tyres and expect to use both. Armed robberies occur on all these roads as people returning from markets with money are often targeted, mugged or killed. In June 1998, my Kivori Poe friends told me, on our way to Kivori Poe in the Kairuku–Hiri district past Bereina, that different sections of the road are 'protected' by different gangs who do not work together. At Kivori Poe I attended a United Church Youth Council Meeting. The purpose of the meeting was to report to the regional body on youth policy, action and problems in the district. Concerns were expressed that there was no strategic plan, no action plan, no follow-ups, no evaluation of initiatives, the Budget 'does not appear to go through correct channels' and a question was posed, 'who does it benefit?' There was debate on village court policy and whether or not it was specific enough to cater for youth needs and suggestions debated as to how youth working on village projects could raise funds. Youth participants expressed their need for practical skills to develop business plans, budget monies and market produce, but youth participation was poor in most districts and one youth group had only six active members. Reasons given were: many young people are bored because they are not learning anything; village chiefs do not understand their problems; and there is no money forthcoming from the national, provincial or local-level governments to repair roads and provide extension services for health care, small business training and market access assistance.

At Woitape in March and May 1998,[1] there was a more positive atmosphere and more active youth participation. The main reason for the more positive atmosphere appeared to be the committed and skilled leadership of the Local Level Government Chairman, Augustine Mac, and the involvement of him and his wife Mary in community and church activities. Mr Mac involved himself with village court magistrates, councillors and chiefs in the arbitration and follow-up of disputes. He believed that for community action to succeed and continue, the community needed to believe in itself, and needed materials and extension support from the Central Province Provincial Government. Woitape producers are plagued by resource deficiencies. While valleys in the district are fertile and good for growing potatoes, strawberries and other fruit and vegetable crops to supply Port Moresby markets, only walking tracks connect valleys and airfreight costs are prohibitive. A village chief from a neighbouring valley had a coffee block planted 'in the colonial times' that he wanted to develop to keep young men at home and away from Port Moresby where they 'get into trouble'. He sought donor funding to build a small road to connect his coffee block with the Woitape airstrip as 'the provincial government did not seem to want to help'.

In an effort to forge links between the provincial government and the local community and to increase resource potential, Mr Mac invited the Governor of Central Province to visit Woitape to open a mini hydroelectric plant, view projects and discuss financial support for future developments. He believed youth occupation in commercial agricultural activity in particular was vital to deterring them from criminal activity in Port Moresby. Some youth groups in the district had taken up the challenge, organising themselves to achieve particular goals. The Uruna village youth group had formed an organisation called the Sika Rescuers 'out of concerns for lawlessness in villages'. A letter written by Catholic Brother, Andrew Anama, on 8 May 1996 to the Woitape Sub-district office on behalf of the Sika Rescuers stated that the group had evolved because 'on many occasions at traditional ceremonies unexpected deaths due to poisoning and belief in sorcery and magical powers' had occurred as well as incidents of rape, adultery and fornication, theft and drug intoxication. A President, Vice-President, Secretary, Treasurer and Committee members were nominated with a view to linking state and community efforts. The committee comprised subsistence farmers, a seminarian, a church councillor, a LLG councillor, a policeman, a teacher and village chiefs. A constitution with 10 elements provided a synopsis of behavioural standards required in the villages with procedures to be adopted if behavioural codes were broken. Village court magistrates, the LLG council chairman and chiefs arbitrated offences considered more serious. The Sika Rescuers had raised a lot of money from fines but the treasurer had 'spent it all' that is, stolen it. The group had learned from this experience and now insisted on more accountability. For example, knowing and seeing how much money there is in the kitty. They had invested in carp farming with their earnings with a view to selling fish to the local community. Youth group identity was strong and there was frequent communication and conjoint action amongst groups in different valleys. For example, youth from district clans and sub-clans, many of whom are 'returned Port Moresby youths who have been rascals', came together to make one large group for work or football. They charged between K10 and K20 for small jobs and up to K50 for large jobs to build fences, houses and gardens. A significant link also appeared to have been forged between police and youth with the local police constable becoming a Sika Rescuer committee member. Yet there was much work to be done on this relationship as LLG councillors said the police and correctional service are not liked because of the way they treat criminals and others. They told the story of a man from Kosipi in the Woitape district who had gone to Port Moresby to buy supplies for an AusAID-funded project. He was with a group of people when the police, who were looking for criminals, started firing. He hid behind a large drum but unfortunately 'popped his head out' at the wrong moment and was shot dead through the forehead. His orders, money and plane ticket were found in his pocket.

In July 1999, I walked the Kokoda Trail with a small group of friends. We flew into Kokoda just over the mountain from where the chief with the coffee block lives and walked back to Port Moresby. It was tough, hot, wet, and very steep in places. Our leader was Narai Billy, a Koirari man, who lives at Sogeri, a 45-minute drive northwest of Port Moresby. Narai had been a voluntary community correctional officer and works closely with youth in his area. He said village communities along the Kokoda Trail are increasingly dependent upon cash for food, healthcare and school fees because many young people have migrated to Port Moresby to work leaving their young children with their grandparents. As a result there is little agricultural activity in the area and Narai tries to employ youth who are left to contribute some cash to communities, paying them K25 a day to carry packs of up to 35 kilograms. Some of 'my boys', he said 'have been rascals' and this work 'keeps them out of trouble'. Unlike foreign-led expeditions that are often attacked 'because they do not stop in villages', we slept in village guesthouses and bought fruit and vegetables at village rest stops. Narai's Kokoda Trail tours were promoted through the PNG Tourist Commission and two employees accompanied us. They said while the commission tries to work with communities and youth groups—conducting awareness workshops on tourist expectations, cultural promotion strategies, and the benefits of tourism—government resource deficiencies had stalled outreach activity. This was concerning, because they believed if sufficient government resources were available for promotion, many more communities could benefit from tourism. Those tourists who would come, have also heard of the robbery and mugging of visitors and prefer instead to spend their tourist dollars in safer places like Fiji.

These anecdotes illustrate the fundamental scarcity of capacity, in terms of human and material resources, of both state agencies and communities to deal with poverty, and hence crime. Where provincial and local-level governments work together and involve citizens in decision making, productivity, commitment and interest are higher. Alarmingly, however, almost all projects are donor funded. An example is the Lae-based Village Development Trust, a non-government organisation working with the Morobe Provincial and Local Level Governments to assist communities to develop eco-forestry, conservation, small-scale business and other ventures towards sustainable development. In 1997 a 69,000 hectare site was gazetted as a Wildlife Management Area for economic development governed by rules enforced by the community-based Kamiali Conservation Committee. The donor-funded project trained young people to become rangers (*Post-Courier* 1 April 1997:15).

The donor-funded North Simbu Rural Development Project was begun in 1994, involved individuals and institutions in activities to increase household income. For example, the local Barawagi prison cultivated coffee seedlings for distribution throughout the province and advisers worked with national, provincial and local-level governments to achieve goals through self-sustaining local initiatives and decentralised district-level planning and decision making. Reported economic outcomes were increased production of smallholder coffee, vegetable production, inland fisheries and sheep and poultry production (Kuble and Godfrid 1999). In March 1999 the 100,000 coffee seedling-capacity nursery at Barawagi prison was supplying seedlings to farmers in marginal areas of North Simbu Province, earning money from sales, training prisoners in nursery work and enhancing prison coffee production.

From May 1995, in West New Britain, the European Union-funded Islands Region Environment and Community Development Programme has worked with staff and inmates at the local Lakiemata prison and surrounding communities developing small-scale community-based timber harvesting enterprises that conserve and manage forest stocks and provide income. Individuals are trained in village-based eco-forestry, the marketing of processed products, and in other community-managed activities including eco-tourism and insect farming, environmental awareness and conservation. A 1997 report by the Washington based Biodiversity Support Program stated '...the large investment in training and equipment...is made possible by the financial support...from the European Union' whose input enables subsidisation of start-up costs of small-scale enterprises (Salafsky 1997:1–2). The West New Britain-based oil palm company, New Britain Palm Oil, maintains the roads to provide market access. Yet no subsidy is forthcoming from the government and the long-term sustainability of the project once the EU withdraws is questionable.

Locally-generated business initiatives also lean on donors for support. In Wewak in May 1997, a young LLG councillor was proactive in developing income-earning opportunities for his community by lobbying foreign donors for funds. Robby Tuta is from the Baniamata Clan on the Sepik River. He attended an SBDC-run business training and bookkeeping course in Wewak, to learn skills to 'keep youth at home by involving them in business activity', as when they went to Wewak they 'got into trouble'. Mr Tuta developed a five-year development plan and obtained UN Development Programme and British High Commission sponsorship for a wildlife management area and artificial lake, a village guesthouse for tourists and cage culture fish farming. Funds to build accommodation for US Peace Corp volunteer specialists in aquaculture were sought and future projects included a women's sewing project, a youth fishing project and lifestyle education in health, nutrition and hygiene (Tuta 1997:1–7). In 1998, the Moresby South Member of Parliament, Lady Carol Kidu, sought AusAID funding to establish micro-financed small business projects for women in NCD urban villages. The purpose of the program was to reinforce the value of self-reliance and accountability and to earn an income. The projects were managed by a non-government organisation that trained participants in basic financial management techniques. Micro-credit schemes for women are also popular in other parts of Papua New Guinea; for example the Western and Eastern Highlands Provinces and in Simbu Province, because most PNG women have low literacy and education levels and no access to credit to start up a business. The schemes enable individual women to borrow up to K300–500 and groups of women to borrow up to K2,000 at an interest rate of 20 per cent. Repayment of loans with interest is crucial to the success of such schemes because repayment of one loan enables another, and if one person fails to repay, another person goes without a loan. Extension support to prepare and train groups in financial management is vital to the success of such schemes but such support is not always available and training is usually donor-funded. The Simbu Province micro-scheme, which began as part of the donor-funded North Simbu Rural Development Project, included enterprises like animal husbandry, vegetable production and *haus-kais* (TP: cooked food stalls). The scheme experienced good loan repayment regimes and there were expectations that loans could be negotiated with commercial banks for bigger business projects involving more people. When aid inputs ceased at the end of 1999, however, only one per cent of Simbu Province women participated (Kuble and Godfrid 1999:16).

While considerable effort has been made by government agencies and community leaders to implement such community development projects, it is greatly concerning that all rely on international donor support—the Village Development Trust, the North Simbu

Development Project, micro-enterprise schemes, Bobby Tuta's village development efforts and the Islands Region Environment and Community Development Program. In relation to the North Simbu Rural Development Project, the International Fund for Agricultural Development loaned K8.49 million, AusAID granted K7.7 million and there was supervisory and technical input from the World Bank, the United Nations Office for Project Services (Asia/Pacific Office), the International Development Support Services Pty Ltd and Care Australia. The project ceased in December 1999 (Kuble and Godfrid 1999), when aid agency withdrawal signalled a downturn in economic activity.

While donors offer reliable resource support to start-up projects and train practitioners, project sustainability beyond the life of donor-funded projects is low. A 1996 review of the UN Development Programme-funded Biodiversity Conservation and Resource Management Programme working with the PNG Department of Environment and Conservation found that while micro-enterprise is believed to be 'the answer' to rural small business development, sustainability rarely occurs beyond the life of projects and is directly related to a lack of government capacity to maintain infrastructure, safe road access to markets, training venues and extension services. The review cited an Enga Province Development Project that had been sustained since the 1980s due only to expatriate volunteer management (Brooks 1996).

Another major inhibitor to small business sustainability is an overall lack of business awareness in communities that host an enterprise. While the SBDC and other government agencies attempt to 'prepare' entrepreneurs and communities for the demands of small business, extension services are severely hampered by insufficient human resources and budgetary allocations. By 1996, SBDC efforts to assist micro-enterprise schemes in the 'preparation phase', had reached only some towns (Brooks 1996). In 1998, extension support of Port Moresby and East Sepik SBDC personnel was confined to 'very occasional small business management courses in towns' due to resource deficiencies. In the case of micro-enterprise, both infrastructure and awareness training of entrepreneurs and communities is crucial—the former to sell produce and earn income, the latter to protect life, limb and property against criminality—because often, business enterprise is at odds with traditional expectations. In traditional PNG societies, those who own or acquire wealth achieve 'big man' status. However to retain such status, 'big men' (and 'big women') must be seen to distribute goods within the community to a degree commensurate with perceived wealth and status. If this does not occur, their leadership or status is challenged and violent attacks can occur upon them and their families (Brooks 1996, King 1997). This ingrained attitude can impede self-help capacity and destroy enterprise. Extension services which work with communities to create awareness of best business practice may, at the very least, minimise the adverse affects of such expectations. Communities educated in best business practice are less likely to be fearful, jealous and ignorant and less likely to act violently towards local entrepreneurs when they feel excluded from economic activity. Conversely, ignorance and fear of reprisals stagnates communities.

Urban settlement entrepreneurs also suffer reprisals if they look too rich or their children appear to be too educated and they do not distribute their wealth according to community expectations. Such reprisals lock others into patterns of drinking and gambling and shunning legitimate work in the belief that they will be attacked, their property destroyed and their earnings stolen if they look too rich. For example, a storeowner in a squatter settlement in Port Moresby who seemed to be 'getting too rich' and 'giving nothing back to the people' had his business looted and burned. A man in another settlement who worked as a handyman and was accumulating wealth was 'chased away' with his wife and their house burned down. In 1999, the Cross Roads Shelter youth rehabilitation project at Taikone village in Port Moresby met a similar fate that may have been avoided had there been intervention by an appropriate extension service. An ex-prisoner, whom I shall call Lincoln, started the project, which went well for over a year before things turned sour. Lincoln expressed concern regarding his lack of business acumen. He called himself 'an ignorant man' and feared this failure would cause confusion and frustration within the group and could destroy it. In lieu of the unavailability of government extension services he approached the German Volunteer Service to run a small business awareness course for the group. A week before the course started Lincoln said 'things were stirring up' and some people were trying to make trouble. He said there was a lot of jealousy in the village about what he was doing and some people, even church elders, were wanting to 'cut him down' telling him he would fail and he was 'just a criminal' and 'the boys are not listening to me anymore and want more and more money'. He hoped the small business course would help to heal a split in the group, but the course did not eventuate. The night before it was scheduled the project office was smashed and burned and Lincoln and some loyal followers 'chased away' on threats of death or sorcery. He was distraught, saying his dreams had been 'smashed by jealousy and ignorance'. A senior public servant remarked of Lincoln's story, 'there is much jealousy in villages' and 'some people use sorcery to keep control'. He said some church elders, who are also powerful sorcerers, maintain autocratic power and undermine those who threaten it, often stymieing efforts to divert youth from crime.[2]

Gavman and *gavman sevises*

Government services are lacking or non-existent in many parts of Papua New Guinea. Roads are in disrepair, in some places impassable, or they are unsafe and travellers are subject to armed robberies, muggings and murder. Agricultural extension, health, education and other services either do not operate or are spasmodic and constantly subject to political wrangling, fraud and insufficient money to pay staff and meet running costs. In this depleted environment, aid-funded programs falter and neglected communities withdraw or express their anger through sabotage. In July 1997, the JICA newsletter overviewed Japanese-sponsored carp farming projects in the Highlands. The projects were designed to boost the protein intake of villagers, increase income-earning potential, train agricultural extension officers and local farmers and promote further research. The report said that while there are many projects in the Eastern Highlands Province, there is little return to local villages and low standards of living prevail because of a lack of infrastructure and because government policy does not correlate with the self-sufficient economic activities of highlands lifestyle (JICA 1997). Flip Van Helden cited a joint National Research Institute/UN Development Programme 1998 report as stating that in relation to development in the Upper Jimi in the Western Highlands Province, and the Ramu Valley in the Morobe Province, people are annoyed at their 'total lack of *gavman sevises*' (TP: government services) including roads, health and schools (Van Helden 1998). Van Helden also cited a report in *The National* on 23 October 1997 in which the people of the Kosap area vented their anger on the new Jimi MP and Western Highlands Administrator because 'no road' meant no education, health and business. Five community schools were without teachers and nine aid posts were without medical staff—teachers and medical staff staying '...in Mount Hagen or their own places...while the children of Kosap are deprived of education and sick people suffer to death'. In the Jimi Valley, perinatal complications and calorie-protein deficiencies in women and children that lower resistance to illness are the main reasons for high mortality in the area (Buchbinder 1973, Wood 1980, United Nations International Children's Fund 1996, Van Helden 1998). Children who live at the Morata settlement in Port Moresby are also deprived of education due to perceived poor discipline within the Department of Education. Morata residents are concerned their children are not getting a good education because teacher school attendance is erratic and some 'get drunk' on their paydays. A parent who complained to the head teacher was informed that if the head teacher tried to discipline teachers, they would threaten and intimidate him. Other parents say they do not want to waste their money on school fees because they are disgusted with the behaviour of teachers and prefer to keep their children at home. When this happens, children become bored, *wokim nogut samting* (TP: make trouble), join criminal gangs, break into houses and destroy property.

Population pressure in Port Moresby urban settlements and villages causes water shortages, sanitation and rubbish disposal problems, resulting in conflicts that often manifest in violence. Local level governments are pressured by both the NCD Commission and communities to provide basic services but are plagued with power struggles. Some urban villagers say their councillors are 'more interested in maintaining their status than helping their communities'. In August 1998 I attended a Motu–Koita Local Level Government Council meeting at Konedobu in Port Moresby. The main item on the agenda was health and the cleanup of Motu–Koita villages. Suggestions were made that the Department of Health conduct an awareness campaign to prompt cleanup of villages, and that K2 penalties be imposed for littering market places and streets. Yet it was discovered that the council could not impose penalties as it was excluded from the Organic Law on provincial and local level governments that allows this. It was therefore decided that responsibility to keep communities clean lay with individual villages or sections of villages, and ward councillors would lead cleanups. A weekly 'Council Day' promoted through the churches was suggested and, to provide 'quality administration', councillors would 'blow a whistle like the *kiap*s used to do for a work day in the village'. NCD Commission promised 44-gallon drums for villagers to deposit rubbish and a tipper truck was to be hired to help youth groups collect the rubbish. Not long after the meeting, the chairman of the council was sacked pending an investigation into misappropriation of funds and only spasmodic cleaning has occurred since.

On 14 June 1999, *The National* reported 'Three provincial govts face probe' in relation to mismanagement and abuse of funds. These are the Fly, Sandaun and Madang Provincial and Local Level Governments. On the same page, there was a report of 'Jobs for sex favours' implicating some senior officers of the Eastern Highlands Provincial Government (*The National* 14 June 1999:6). On 4 November 1999, it was reported that two top government officials from Western Province faced prosecution for alleged involvement in criminal activities. The allegations related to 'misuse of K10,000' and 'conspiring in drug smuggling' (*The National* 4 November 1999:4). On 28 January 2000, it was reported that the Western Province Governor and several senior officials had been charged with misappropriation. The allegations were that the Governor misappropriated K122,046.69, using it to pay individuals and companies and to pay for school fees, funeral expenses, leave entitlements, personal household items and furniture and 'other irregular and extravagant expenses'. The Deputy Governor, former Administrator, Provincial Treasurer, President of a Local Level Government Council, Provincial Executive Council officer, a security guard and a driver were also implicated in relation to misuse of public monies of K40,000, K25,000, K20,000, two amounts of K10,000 and K4,000, respectively, and the Executive Director of the Governor's office was alleged to have misappropriated and conspired to defraud the state of K1.93 million (*Post-Courier* 28 January 2000:3). Two years before the alleged corruption of Western Province leaders, Aberagerema villagers in the South Fly District and Yau villagers in the Middle Fly District of Western Province had understandably expressed disbelief that government promises would manifest in services or development action. Both communities were plagued with poor health services, frequent maternal and infant deaths and illness, little safe water, poor sanitation, minimal access to education, lawlessness and criminal activities by young people who are uneducated and have nothing to do (Office of National Planning 1999b). A 1997 Auditor-General's Report on District Support Grants found in relation to the Gulf Province that there was serious negligence in keeping records and suggested that gross corrupt and fraudulent activity occurred, in particular: weaknesses in the maintenance of Receiver of Public Monies Account, deficiencies in the maintenance of Treasury Operating Account, non-compliance with procurement and payment procedures, deficiencies in the management of District Support Grants, inadequate control over other grants and subsidies, inadequate control over payment and acquittal of advances, shortcomings in payment of salaries and wages and internal control weaknesses. No action appears to have been taken, however. Two years later on 25 January 2000, the *Post-Courier* reported further allegations of financial abuse and mismanagement of public funds by a senior officer in the Gulf Province Administration totalling more than K500,000. The allegations included excessive borrowing of thousands of kina from the Provincial Treasury, abuse of school subsidy funds, abuse of disaster funds, unbudgeted overseas travel, excessive 'finger-dipping' by the provincial government's business arm and payments to a 'concubine' in Port Moresby. Attempts had not been made to have outstanding advances acquitted or made good and (in spite of the 1997 Auditor-General's Report) 'the officer keeps pressing the treasury staff to pay him allowances and advances for his continuous travels' and two advances totalling K23,000 paid to him were 'spent in two or three days' (*Post-Courier* 25 January 2000:2).

In 1998, the UN Development Programme funded the Office of National Planning to conduct Participatory Rural Appraisals in 16 villages throughout Papua New Guinea. A Human Development Report was produced which revealed a common theme of community perceptions of marginalisation and expressions of related resentment. During the appraisal exercise, targeted communities worked with Office of National Planning staff to identify key issues regarding the development of their communities. Common needs in participating communities included schools, cash to pay for school fees, health services, transport to send produce to markets, easier and safer access to markets, assistance to utilise land better to produce more food, and better protection against criminality (Office of National Planning 1999b). In the context of providing development to control crime, state capacity to provide resources for development is often limited by political interference, poor leadership, lack of accountability and corruption. For example, the Chief of all Chiefs at Kivori Poe in the Kairuku–Hiri District of Central Province was scathing in his criticism of government agencies. He said while LLG councillors consult him regarding development projects for youth, the money never comes, the highway remains in very poor condition (some parts have now been upgraded), police come to see him only when there are problems, the health clinic, started several years ago remains unfinished (because the K10,000 promised by the provincial government did not arrive), village youth have no respect for the property of others and steal food, commit highway robbery, drift into Port Moresby, join gangs, go to jail or get killed. The Participatory Rural Appraisal at Rarai Village adjacent to Kivori Poe, had similar problems emanating from power struggles between chiefs and councillors, elders and youths that disrupted village harmony and led to water shortages, sanitation problems, poor nutrition, frequent illness, a lack of technical support to start up enterprises, a lack of credit availability and lack of provision of market outlets. Understandably, many Port Moresby rascals come from the Kairuku–

Hiri District. A long-term prisoner from Cape Rodney in the Abau district believed providing skills development for youth and government services to village communities would help to solve the crime problem and keep young people away from Port Moresby. The Participatory Rural Appraisal at Maopa Village in the Abau district also revealed that the Maopa community sought government assistance to provide technical support to start up enterprise, financial support and market outlets to reduce lawlessness (Office of National Planning 1999b).

In lieu of legitimate channels to obtain cash, general lack of support from all levels of government and poor crime control, marijuana production has flourished. The *Post-Courier* headlined on 11 May 2000 'Marijuana vice deeply rooted', the article stating that Papua New Guinea serves a large domestic and international market with the value of locally-cultivated marijuana trading for up to K300 per kilogram. Many agricultural producers grow marijuana. In some areas it provides a form of exchange for food and other items but children as young as seven or eight years are regular users (Hiambohn 2000d). In this high-need and under-resourced environment, the reality is that crime cannot be controlled. The facts are that 20,000 unemployed youth enter the labour market each year, only 52 per cent of PNG citizens are literate, many citizens die before the age of 40 from preventable illness, and only 24 per cent of people have access to safe water. Given that only 2.6 per cent of Papua New Guinea's gross national product is spent on health and education—73 infants and 31 children die for every 1,000 born, almost 1,000 women die per 100,000 births from preventable pregnancy-related illness, women are less educated and less literate than men and receive only 16 per cent of the national income (UN Development Programme 1998). Sick, uneducated, desperate and disillusioned people cannot sustain development initiatives and do not feel guilty about obtaining resources in illicit ways when they are unavailable otherwise.

Beyond the struggle for good health and education in Papua New Guinea, is the struggle for economic participation. Economists grapple with reasons why greater economic participation does not occur—the belief being that such participation will deter youth from crime. Criminals and communities say they want economic development and say they would participate more with technical, financial and logistical support from the government. The need is illustrated by the fact that in 1997, out of 337 Port Moresby individuals, 69.2 per cent of males who considered themselves 'unemployed' were 'employed' in criminal activities (Levantis 1997). Mawuli and Dzuali made similar discoveries in their 1993 survey of six communities in Port Moresby; in particular that 62 per cent of Nine Mile settlement residents were 'unemployed' (Mawuli and Dzuali 1993:1–13). They recommended that government policy focus on the promotion and creation of self-employment and small business by providing technical and financial assistance to enhance economic participation. They saw this as crucial because low education levels, non-availability of menial jobs, apprenticeships and vocational school education, keep many young people jobless. However the hard line taken in relation to the informal sector, which has resulted in the aggressive dispersal of street vendors in centres like Port Moresby, simply destroys legitimate income earning opportunities for unskilled youth who are otherwise drawn into crime (Levantis 2000).

While Waiko agrees that better availability of education and more paid employment would help, he says that for most Papua New Guineans there is a conflict between village and modern societies, resulting in personal struggles to meet both sets of demands. Most people are keen to have their identity and competency recognised in both the traditional and modern arenas but straddling these arenas can be difficult because of their different expectations (Waiko 1993). For example, a young woman whose brother was jailed for murder, said there is considerable friction within families and clans when illiterate village parents or leaders remain unaware of the influences on youth of modern education and urban lifestyle and they continue to take a traditional, authoritarian approach to discipline. In the urban environment, youth acquire a new cultural orientation and such authoritarianism can push adolescents out of school and into criminality to avoid losing face amongst peers. Rarai youth believe their chiefs do not understand them. Their plight is widespread: authoritarianism, bullying and shaming is prevalent, common and expected in many PNG communities. Youths want to please both traditional and modern arenas but school leavers have expectations of paid employment to enable them to gain traditional social status through their ability to contribute to economic obligations. If such expectations are not fulfilled, loss of traditional pride and dignity occurs and frustration and anger can manifest in criminal activity to obtain 'Western goods' (Waiko 1993). Opportunities of earning legitimate income, however, do not always result in an enthusiastic response. For example, a Port Moresby settlement dweller was assisted by the local landowner to start up an ice cream business. Other residents were offered coconuts to sell to pay for school fees. Both ventures failed because of jealousy and ignorance and the money earned was spent on betel nut, beer parties or gambled, and the children were left to 'run wild' and 'beg for food'. In an effort to 'keep the kids off the streets' the landowner built a bush materials house from *kunai* grass and old packing cases. She called it *Haus Man* (TP: Men's house). The structure became a venue for settlement children to play, sleep and occasionally to eat, to prevent them from wandering the streets and stealing. Two had already been killed on the busy road bordering the property. The *Haus Man* was 'officially opened' and blessed by the local pastor whose church sits in the settlement. A pig was killed, vegetables cooked, while 30 hungry children waited patiently with their enamel and plastic food bowls. Distribution of the food was monitored carefully and contrary to tradition, children were fed first (the Christmas before, when the landowner killed a pig in celebration, the adults ate all the food).

Practical education to provide skills to youth is a commonly expressed need. Vocational schools, usually church-run, have taken up this challenge. Yet most are under-resourced and struggle to operate. Government subsidies are meagre and always late and most survive on the charity of overseas parishes or occasional donor contributions. One impressive establishment in Port Moresby is the Catholic-run Maino Heduru Youth Centre known as 'the mission school' at Erima, in Port Moresby. In Motu, *Maino* means peace and *Heduru* means self-help. The school is run by four Australian Catholic nuns of the Brigadine Order who receive no wages and depend upon the charity of their 'sisters' in Australia for sustenance. They are dedicated, strong-willed and have a vision for PNG youth.

On 4 December 1998, I attended the graduation of their grade nine students, aged mainly between 13 and 18 years. None of the graduates had been able to go to high school because their families could not afford the fees or there were insufficient places. During their three years with the nuns, students were taught cooking, sewing, woodwork and metalwork, keyboard skills, English and mathematics. Most are born in Port Moresby but are culturally heterogenous and represent most Christian faiths. Some parents and guardians attended, many did not. The children sang hymns, gave speeches and sang goodbye songs. I asked Sister Kathleen what would become of them. She said some girls would get jobs, others would get pregnant or get married while many boys would return to rascalism as there was nothing else for them to do and they had to eat. All could study through CODE if they could afford K70 per subject, but many of course could not. The school principal, a small, frail sister called Morris gave a sobering speech. She said, 'we are looking for young national staff to take over from us. I'm not a spring chicken', and 'I won't be able to go on for much longer'. She said national teachers who worked at the school did so 'mainly from the goodness of their hearts' as they were paid only K100 per fortnight. 'Who', she asked, 'would take over at these rates of pay?' and the government subsidy of only K25 per student 'didn't even pay the electricity bill'. The school has now been approved as a vocational school which means it should attract greater government subsidy and teacher support.[3]

Leadership integrity is linked with resource availability, the achievement of development objectives and the prevention of crime. However, there are government delays and there is community marginalisation. In East New Britain, two elderly councillors led a group of youths on a rampage through St Mary's high school at Vunakanau because of 'the mistreatment of local people by the headmaster'. In the Western Highlands Province councillors representing local villagers stole five high-powered rifles from police, who were guarding the Mt Kegum Telikom repeater station, because thieves took their guns (*Post-Courier* 8 May 2000:2, 18 May:4). In Simbu Province, villagers who felt marginalised by government over delayed or unresolved compensation claims in relation to land on which telecommunication transmitters stood, sabotaged the equipment. As a consequence Barawagi, the province's prison, has been without telephones for several years. In June 1999, Kerevat prison in East New Britain was under threat of land claims. The Kairak Clan had claimed ownership because clan members felt cheated of their land under a 'colonial' agreement, agricultural expansion was now required because clan numbers had increased, and 'inflation justifies more compensation'. At the same time, the East New Britain Provincial Government and Gazelle Restoration Authority were not providing education, health and other services, nor were they upgrading roads, nor was the prison commander employing clan members as casual staff in the prison.

In 1994, an incident occurred on the outskirts of Port Moresby which bespoke of marginalisation and broken promises by leaders. It was the subject of a study by Sinclair Dinnen in 'Praise the Lord and pass the ammunition' (1994b:23). He observed that marginalised groups create 'negotiating space with those in political and economic power' with a view to opening up 'new opportunities for individual and collective advancement'. I was informed of the incident in May 1999. My informer had lived at Sabusa near Laloki where the incident had occurred and worked off and on with gangs who wanted to give up crime and participate in legitimate activity. Along with others, he negotiated with criminal justice agencies, politicians and senior public servants for an amnesty on firearms that resulted in gangs surrendering their weapons to police. An agreement was struck between the government and gangs after some months of talks. The government agreed to assist gangs in and around Sabusa to start up a small business if they gave up criminality. Three projects were identified including poultry and timber. The accounting firm Deloitte assisted gangs to write proposals that were sent to relevant government Ministers. The gangs waited. They received no reply to their proposals. They waited longer and lobbied Ministers for another six months. Not one government Minister followed up with them. Gang members lost interest, became aggressive and threatened my informer and his family with murder and rape for 'not doing enough'. He and his family fled. The gangs returned to criminality.

These examples indicate the unreliability of some government leaders to fulfil promises and provide resources—such unreliability is a key issue governing development project outcomes that may divert criminal activity. The examples also indicate that some leaders do not translate rhetoric and policy into action and resources, preferring instead to rely on donor agency support or to do nothing, and to ignore the gross allegations of corruption and mismanagement against them.

Fraud prevention

Arundhati Roy states that if human beings had the inherent morality assumed by Nehru and Gandhi, achieved by suppressing base urges, then developing positive perceptions and actions for the greater common good would be easier. She concedes however that this is not the case generally and that a breaking of faith in what could or should be, instead concentrating on what actually is, may be a beginning to fighting specific wars in specific ways with a view to achieving a result (Roy 1999). Papua New Guinea's Foreign Minister, Sir John Kaputin, stated at a conference on Asia-Pacific governance that the survival of individuals, communities and nations depends upon rules that regulate proper behaviour and rules that are respected. He said respect for rules is 'a matter of political will' beyond the 'inspiring words' of leaders, that manifest in the commitment of officials at every level and every branch of government and actively involves ordinary people (Kaputin 2000:11). Bonnell points out however that the dilemma in Papua New Guinea is that most Papua New Guineans prefer to restore harmony and patch up poor relations through restitution and compensation, rather than punish perpetrators through the formal criminal justice system (Bonnell 1999). Combating the high level of corruption and citizen neglect that now exists in Papua New Guinea would seem to require a much stronger approach. Papua New Guinea is now part of the global community, whose membership dictates particular rules and regulations and standards of behaviour in relation to human rights. PNG plunderers of the public purse have entered the international arena by allegedly depositing their illicit earnings in foreign bank accounts and buying

Table 8 Prevention and punishment of fraud: Office of Rural Development Draft Fraud Control Plan

Fraud prevention	Fraud punishment
Initiate fraud education and awareness to ensure each individual understands what fraud is, his/her roles and responsibilities, reporting procedures, and are made aware of updates and changes to fraud-related policies, procedures, codes of conduct, and ethics. Ensure fraud control measures, activities and other information are distributed to staff. Ensure each individual adheres to policies, procedures, and codes of conduct. Ensure Fraud Liaison Officers are appointed. Ensure Security Officers know their roles and responsibilities. Appoint a Departmental Fraud Control Sub-Committee. If an individual suspects fraud, ensure he/she knows to note observations, report concerns, inform only those who need to know. Report matter to the nominated Department Fraud Liaison Officer, or if lacking confidence in management to deal with the matter, fear of implication in suspected fraudulent activity, or fear of reprisals: make complaints to the Ombudsman. Ensure individuals know their duty to assist police. Make sure the police inform informants of their rights first, or Seek the services of a solicitor for representation.	Under the Public Service (Management) Act, individuals suspected of fraud, can be suspended with or without pay once circumstances of fraud are known officially. Prosecution policy for all cases of suspected fraud requires development. Recovery of all benefits of fraudulent activity needs to be pursued vigorously.

Source: Office of Rural Development 2000. *Draft Fraud Control Plan*, Government of Papua New Guinea, March:3–7.

foreign property (Manning 2000b:11). These actions are beyond local social mores and draw appropriate sanctions from the government and the international community.

With a view to controlling fraud by politicians and public servants the Office of Rural Development initiated two innovative mechanisms: the draft Fraud Control Plan and a working draft of the District Development Program Social and Rural Development Grant Guidelines (Social and Rural Development Grant Guidelines) for the fiscal year 2000 (see Tables 8 and 9).

Table 8 shows that the Fraud Control Plan includes a Fraud Prevention Strategy, and defines fraud and corrupt practice as 'a range of deceitful acts that people commit to benefit themselves or others at the expense of the state'. It includes the provision of sensitive information to third parties without authorisation, doing 'special favours' for an agency or person, contrary to open, fair and effective competition, taking or using public property or resources without approval, stealing and/or misusing property and payment claims for unperformed services. The plan specifies corrupt practice as bribery, conflicts of interest, breaches of confidence, unethical behaviour, information security and information peddling, and clearly defines 'obtaining a benefit' or 'avoiding an obligation'. These acts include theft of cash or attractive and valuable items, obtaining secret commissions, gifts or 'kick-backs' such as hospitality and accommodation discounts, sponsored travel and entertainment, getting early payments or advances, obtaining approvals under false pretences or avoiding contractual obligations, providing false or incomplete information, falsifying records, claiming allowances to which the recipient is not entitled or avoiding proper procedure (Office of Rural Development 2000a).

Table 9 shows that the draft District Development Program Social and Rural Development Grant Guidelines seek to address specific community development needs through accountable leader and community involvement—to ensure the K89 million allocated annually to districts for infrastructure projects is targeted, controlled and managed to maximise service delivery to people. It details the steps and procedures involved in the utilisation and accounting of the Social and Rural Development Grant funds and documents the

Table 9 Eligible and ineligible projects: Social and Rural Development Grants

Eligible projects	Ineligible projects
Transport infrastructure: roads, feeder roads, bridges, airstrips, wharves (total cost of each not exceeding K300,000). District Administration infrastructure: housing for key staff, including treasurer, administrator and planner as well as police, CS, and other related extension personnel. Health infrastructure: aid-posts and clinics, health worker housing, rural water supply. Education infrastructure: elementary and primary school classroom construction and teacher housing.	Payment for goods that will be privately used/owned. Illegal or immoral activities and such related purposes. Payment of bride price, funeral costs and similar. Travel expenses of a personal nature and procurements for own use. Investments in businesses or equity purchases. Securities or collateral for loans purposes. Political party expenses. Other activities and such purposes not in line with Government's development policies or contravene existing policies and regulations. Social capital formation (training courses, technical consultancies, study tours, and so on). Transport, agricultural or contsruction equipment. Office and computer equipment.

Equity test
Projects dispersed throughout wards within district unless justified on district wide benefit grounds.
Project approval to consider equity.
LLG councils in district to benefit from projects within a two-year cycle.
No LLG council is to gain more than 25 per cent of funds in any one year.
Exceptions
In districts with less than four LLG councils
In special circumstances where there is province wide benefit
No acceptable projects proposals are received from an LLG council.

Source: Office of Rural Development, 2000. *Working Draft of the District Development Program Social and Rural Development Grant Guidelines for the Fiscal Year 2000,* Government of Papua New Guinea, March:9–10.

physical progress of projects funded under the grant. In particular, it outlines the purpose of district development, guidelines, eligible and ineligible projects, entities eligible to submit proposals, procedures for submissions and approval and financial accountability and management of funds (Office of Rural Development 2000b). The Ombudsman Commission's AusAID-funded Leadership through Accountability Project also appears to have the potential to be a worthwhile method to control crime by starting a process towards greater accountability in relation to Parliamentarians' Discretionary Funds. In a letter dated 21 December 1999, to all Members of Parliament, the Chief Ombudsman, Simon Pentanu, sought the assistance of parliamentarians to 'improve the scheme so that it better achieves its objectives' in response 'to the needs and aspiration of the people' and 'to help the improvement of the work of governmental bodies and to supervise the enforcement of the Leadership Code'.

While the Office of Rural Development Fraud Plan and Social and Rural Development Grant guidelines are mechanisms that may reduce corrupt practice by politicians and public servants, their practice beyond inspiring words will be 'a matter of political will'. Sir John Kapautin suggests that to produce results, political will must translate into courage and into resource availability to prosecute and punish offenders, sending a clear message to citizens that such behaviour is unacceptable and not tolerated (Kaputin 2000). John Nonggorr lamented there are 'inquiries galore—but no action' and to move forward as a nation the past must be cleaned up to 'set the stage for the future' (Nonggorr 1999:15). Governor-General Sir Silas Atopare says the objective of public sector reform is to make governments more accountable so that public administrators can fulfil their goals of equity, fairness, due process and accountability to the people who have elected them (Togarewa 1998). In practice, individuals must be informed, delegated, monitored and checked to ensure adherence to due process that creates equity, fairness and accountability. Best management practice that leads to greater resource availability and to the exposure and prosecution of fraudulent offenders is a powerful method of crime control because from it, citizens learn the value of discipline and order and are empowered by it. With widespread adoption of best management practice, an informed, courageous, proactive public emerges that demands accountability and is willing to make sacrifices to achieve it because it has experienced the value of it. The long-term result of greater equity and fairness is historically a reduction in crime. However the adoption of best practice is not happening in Papua New Guinea and as already discussed, sick, uneducated, uninformed citizens are powerless or fearful to act. Therefore, while a Law and Order Policy has been developed that advocates strengthening the capacity of criminal justice agencies and encouraging community participation in decision making, its implementation is prevented by lack of dedicated resource support from the government.

In 1997, PNG politician Chris Haiveta stated that Papua New Guinea's international image improvement will come not from any social improvements to domestic standards of living, but rather from improvements in macroeconomic management (Haiveta 1997:xxii). However, macroeconomic management cannot improve until the behaviour of political and institutional leaders improves through transparency, audit, regulation and punishment. International investors and aid agencies watch PNG's performance in relation to its human development indicators and its integrity in repaying debts. When the country continues to rank 133 out of 174 countries in social development indicators—in spite of the enormity of aid input—the international community wonders what PNG politicians are doing with the money they are supposed to be managing and wonders whether or not money loaned will be paid back (*Post-Courier* 16 May 2000:3).

Conclusion

This chapter resonates the theme that until the PNG Government develops the capacity to exercise greater political and fiscal discipline to ensure resources reach those who need them, most innovative policies to develop communities and control crime will founder. This is because community attempts to prevent and control crime and maintain order are irretrievably linked with state capacity, which is itself dictated by the quality of leadership and the way that quality translates into the provision of resources for citizens. The sustainability of community-based development initiatives, not supported by government extension services, is often thwarted by resource difficulties or community ignorance, fear, jealousy and bigotry. Communities who do not understand enterprise and feel marginalised by it often react violently towards entrepreneurs—causing development failure. Minimal government commitment to provide financial and infrastructure support also hampers development and creates unhealthy long-term dependency upon donors.

Papua New Guinea communities commonly express concern regarding poor nutrition, high maternal and infant mortality rates, general poor health and short life spans. Sick and hungry people do not work well. Uneducated and unemployed youth disrupt communities and eventually join criminal gangs for status and prestige and to provide for their families. Communities express their need for basic services like education, health, clean water, sanitation, safe roads and extension support before development initiatives can be achieved. They say they want leaders who steal public monies punished and they want their leaders to show integrity and commitment, by translating promises into policy and into resources to enhance their safety, their quality of life, their educational opportunities and their opportunities to earn cash income.

Notes

1 The Woitape District borders the Goilala District and is inland from the Kairuku-Hiri District.

2 Lincoln's business has since re-emerged.

3 In August 2001, the Australian nuns were ordered to return to Australia for their own safety. They had been attacked repeatedly by criminals in their insecure lodgings at the school.

7
Crime, corruption and capacity

Crime control methods in Papua New Guinea are based upon shared values and opinions often politically influenced, biased and prompted by fear of negative sanctions, reducing their capacity to protect the rights of citizens. Within the cultural diversity of the country, crime control methods vary from community to community, from court to court, from police station to police station, from prison to prison. The diversity applies to an array of methods including: warnings and apprehension by police, prison sentences, fines or community-based options from courts, rehabilitation strategies by the A-GD and PNGCS, village court hearings and punishments, behaviour monitoring by peace officers, arbitration by village chiefs, other leaders and church elders, the creation of practical learning and economic opportunities for unemployed youth to divert them from crime, and the formation of youth and vigilante groups.

Papua New Guinea politicians have eloquent rhetoric concerning the eradication of crime. The press documents lengthy screeds by leaders goading communities to help police with inquiries, report crime and utilise state methods to arbitrate conflicts. There is much talk and coverage of corruption, including misappropriation of public funds, deception and fraud, together with deliberations by politicians, senior public servants, church leaders, women's leaders, journalists, academics and the general public on the importance of bringing perpetrators in positions of trust to justice. Many promises are made to prosecute and punish leaders who allegedly commit fraud. Yet beyond Commissions of Inquiry, few prosecutions ensue, and even fewer perpetrators are punished, because under-resourced agencies either fail to apprehend or to prosecute criminals. Bribes, intimidation, threats, muggings, rapes and killings stymie the most courageous efforts of criminal justice practitioners. When pressured to meet political agendas to 'do something', criminal justice agencies often respond with reactive and brutal force that further alienates communities. This is paradoxical because criminal justice agency staff are also community members—members of extended families increasingly connected cross-culturally and including at least one member who is a criminal and others deprived of health clinics, medicines, schools, teachers, books and roads. At the same time, court and parole board backlogs cause prison overcrowding and community-based sentencing options are not tenable in under-resourced environments. Both criminal justice agency staff and communities experience deprivation caused by scarce resources and express anger in relation to it. To further complicate interactions, many criminal justice agency staff work in or close to their own ethnic communities and are thus often caught up in family conflicts and traditional obligations.

Papua New Guineans have a strong sense of community with a preference to conciliate disputes and compensate victims rather than punish perpetrators. Given this, and the informal interaction that occurs between criminal justice agency staff and communities, it would appear that the most cost-effective option to control petty crime is to give responsibility for control to communities. Ideally, leaders can then arbitrate socially acceptable compensation to avoid further disputes and orchestrate strategies to rehabilitate offenders. The village court system was set up for this purpose and remains central to community conflict resolution as it gives communities the opportunity to participate in decision making based upon shared values and opinions. At the same time, the system provides a structure designed to preserve the rights of citizens as enshrined in the PNG Constitution. While many citizens say they prefer to settle disputes through village courts, they also say some village court officials are ill-trained, ill-paid and ill-resourced, interpret and apply legislation poorly, discriminate severely against women, and hand down biased sentences.

Creating incentives for youth to learn practical skills and earn legitimate income also appears to be an ideal way of depleting the pool of unemployed youth from which gang leaders draw criminal lackeys. However, communities deprived of education and health services, with no access to capital and markets, and who receive no support from government extension services, have no means of sustaining incentives. Community leaders express their sadness, helplessness and anger as their bored, uneducated youth migrate to cities, join criminal gangs, go to jail or get killed. They become passively resistant to state goading when politicians tell them they must assist police to apprehend criminals who are their sons, brothers, nephews and cousins. When grand words fail to translate into resource support, protecting their young criminals, or capitalising on the desires of vote-driven politicians, appears more materially advantageous than helping the police to catch their relatives, or waiting for government distribution systems—blocked by corrupt practice and poor management—to provide. In this needy environment, both morally deficient politicians and criminal leaders thrive. Politicians, as patrons of deprived communities, are assured of votes to remain in the *bisnis* of politics. Criminal gang leaders, confident of community protection, orchestrate increasingly sophisticated and vicious crime, drawing indulgently from the pool of poor, unemployed, uneducated youth for front line work. While short-term material benefits are realised by some communities, others receive nothing. The consequent repercussions of crime are fear, disincentive and an estimated direct cost to PNG taxpayers each year of K90 million. (The opportunity cost of crime, or the value of development that would happen in the absence of it, is much, much greater.) Corrupt politicians, who manipulate resource distribution to satiate their greed, trap their constituents in uninformed limbo, blocking development initiatives that could facilitate some very worthwhile community crime control strategies.

It cannot be denied that Australian and German colonialists entered a rich and diverse society when they claimed Papua and New Guinea in 1884. And it cannot be denied that in 1975, Australian colonialists left Papua New Guinea a legacy of weak, fragmented, inappropriate and inadequate political and legal systems with a few educated indigenous elite to administer them. With over 700 culturally diverse language groups to govern, in a country with a geographically impenetrable hinterland, early administrators floundered in the face of scarce resources. Before and after Independence, cronyism and nepotism grew in an already archaic, unmanageable administrative regime, and while PNG communities wanted to understand more about the 'power' of Western ways, most were given insufficient information to do so. The introduced British system of laws therefore appeared weak, confusing and convoluted and many local leaders who were excluded from debate relating to its instillation, believed it undermined their power and attempted to sabotage it. Communication gaps increased between the state and communities regarding the new laws, their value and application. As the Australian administration gradually withdrew prior to independence, resource support to administer and inform communities was also withdrawn—some people believed it was inadequate anyway. As a result of resource withdrawal, many communities became isolated and detached from the state and were left to juggle two laws; the state law and the underlying law that recognised custom—the two philosophies and perceptions of crime and the application of punishment, often conflicting.

Papua New Guinea's one per cent of educated élite struggled to create national unity in the face of rapid social and economic change, an exploding population, a stagnant economy, political fragmentation due to a lack of collective vision, and reduced state resource capacity. Economic divisions between rich and poor expanded, and vast pools of unemployed, uneducated youth were created by rapid urban migration of persons in search of goods and services. Resources to rural areas shrank gradually in the first post-Independence decade, declined further thereafter and thrust more migrants into the cities. Corruption flourished and continues to do so. The media reports blatant and sophisticated abuse of powers by politicians, their unaccounted spending of slush fund millions, their buying of votes, and their use of violence to oppose decisions that harm their economic interests. Criminal gang leaders exploit government instability, utilising reciprocity networks in the guise of 'traditional exchange' to maximise illicit benefits. Politicians and public servants caught up in this chain reaction exercise selective, rather than effective, crime control strategies with a view to keeping all major players on side.

Increasingly, crime is better planned and targeted for political or economic advantage, while the poor and vulnerable are often victims of vicious crime prompted by substance abuse, ethnic bias or ethnic conflict. At the same time, more than half the crimes reported are not cleared. The extent of the problem is illustrated by the fact that Papua New Guinea tops 58 countries in reported non-economic and violent crimes, and ranks second in the world for sexual violence against women. Researchers believe that, in addition to approximately 11,500 crimes reported annually, up to 70 per cent of crimes perpetrated are not reported to police, resolved instead through 'traditional' methods of compensation and gift giving according to the perceived wealth and status of patrons and perpetrators. The Sandline crisis is a good example of well-planned crime, and a good example of the avarice of some politicians and public servants. It had an enormous, single impact on undermining community confidence in State integrity, especially when fraudulent perpetrators of the public purse—identified by two Commissions of Inquiry—were not prosecuted and retained their power and their wealth. By this gross inaction, the value of cheating was reinforced, socio-economic inequalities were highlighted, communities were further marginalised and more petty offenders have become the scapegoats of an unequal legal system.

Despite this folly, and with a view to solving economic and social problems, aid agencies continue to pour millions of kina into a stricken PNG economy. The view of AusAID, Papua New Guinea's biggest donor, is that if it persists for long enough, governance will improve through structural reform, informed decision making, greater accountability, and attitudinal and behavioural change at senior levels. Yet donors cannot do the work and fix the problems. This is the responsibility of the government. The Prime Minister, Sir Mekere Morauta, is doing his best to achieve greater accountability and attitudinal and behavioural change through disciplining his Ministers, introducing economic and structural reforms and a political integrity law. However his fellow politicians and departmental heads continually undermine his efforts, fail to make dedicated commitments in practical terms to development projects, and fail to inform citizens of legislation, financial status of public accounts and progress. As a consequence, citizens fail to support government initiatives and instead, mirror the behaviour of leaders, who are in constant conflict with one another, avoid punishment for gross wrongdoings and remain wealthy and intractable. Aid project outcomes are undermined when politicians and senior public servants disregard due process—negating all efforts to create public sector environments of reliable and informed leadership. While public sector reform is proffered to streamline practise and dispense with human resource 'deadwood', little positive organisational change can occur unless appropriate learning environments are established to educate public servants and the general public in legislation, due process, rights and responsibilities. Visions, missions, goals and policies developed by criminal justice agencies will be in vain unless resources to government agencies and provincial and local level governments increase in real terms. Resources are needed to target strategies that consistently provide for, train and value staff across ethnic and micro interest group boundaries and utilise systems of accountability to prosecute and punish perpetrators. Similarly, if reforms are too ambitious and not linked with available resources they will fail, and the passivity or brutal reactions of law enforcers will continue. The 1999 Law and Order policy which advocates greater community participation in decision making appears socially and economically cost-effective in the long term. In the short term, however, it is reliant upon political will and public service human and material resource input for implementation. While staff are demoralised and funds are not forthcoming, the policy will inevitably stall.

The ingrained neglect of Papua New Guinea's citizens by politicians and government agencies alienates communities. While a village court system has been established to link formal and informal controls, in reality, the system functions poorly and unpaid court officials who often double as councillors, church elders and sorcerers are tempted to distort legislation to maintain power. Poorly-resourced and supported community correctional officers cannot do their jobs, and prison commanders—keen to rehabilitate prisoners—spend their time 'begging' for food to feed prisoners and petrol to run vehicles. Most criminal justice agency staff abhor the corrupt and negligent practice of some of their leaders, but most choose to do nothing in the interests of self-protection, to keep their jobs and avoid 'the firearms'. By doing nothing, however, they effectively condone such behaviour. This indolent and troubled criminal justice sector reduces the capacity of both the state and communities to initiate and sustain crime control strategies. Community capacity relies on healthy, literate, informed, confident and transparent people to absorb, believe in and apply new ideas. At the same time, government capacity relies on healthy, literate, educated, informed, confident and transparent public servants—with sufficient expertise, materials and equipment—to provide resource support to communities. When governments are indolent, communities become indolent. In being indolent, communities achieve their own victimisation by failing to demand what they really want; that is, higher moral and ethnical standards from their leaders, manifested in consistent and equitable distribution of goods and services.

Often, PNG leaders and citizens say they prefer the 'Melanesian way' to the democratic way through which to resolve conflicts and grievances. This may include gift giving, compensation or paying back a grievance with violence. Outcomes are not always equitable and the universal values of honesty and integrity are often eroded and transformed into behaviour that capitalises through the *bisnis* of politics. When this occurs, the 'Melanesian way' is exposed as a soft term for fraud, nepotism and cronyism that denies citizens their rights. It blocks affirmative action against weak, insecure regimes and manipulates goods and service delivery to citizens desperate for resources. Citizens, uninformed of the value of due process and the destabilising effect of the 'Melanesian way' on public sector performance, may condone bribes for favours and other illicit behaviour. As a consequence, criminal justice agencies suffer low morale and low productivity. Practitioners scratch out a professional existence with little or no support or recognition and are forced to exploit opportunities for advancement in ways that may not always be legitimate. Communities are denied adequate protection and offenders—whose cases are stalled by court and parole board consideration and who have few rehabilitative opportunities—frequently escape from prisons.

While aid agencies work with the criminal justice sector to assist practitioners to strengthen administrative and operational capacity, commitment within agencies to the development process is piecemeal. At the aid project design stage, assumptions are made regarding agency absorptive capacity. These assumptions are grounded in the opinions of agency leaders who, desirous of drawing aid money and not wishing to lose face, may omit the underlying political and administrative incumbrances that block agency capacity to implement new ideas. Design and implementation, review, trial and modification of aid projects that allow for underlying incumbrances takes time, more time than is currently allocated. Extended time to design, trial and evaluate strategies in ways that take account of the less obvious underlying inhibitions would result in more cost-effective programs that save donors substantial sums of money. Moreover, more thoughtful design; that is, design more in tune with organisational political, social and cultural mores, would form a stronger base to create solutions that achieve agreed outcomes, and combat the underlying negative influences that prolong dependency upon expatriate managers and advisers. Weak state government agencies impact on aid effectiveness to support crime control strategies, regardless of good project design. For either state or community controls to work, state agencies need to be strong rather than weak, well-managed rather than neglected, highly productive rather than ineffective and transparent rather than opaque.

Disillusioned, sick, uneducated, uninformed people cannot, and do not want to control crime if criminal acts provide them with resources that governments do not. In 2001, Papua New Guinea ranked 133 out of 174 countries on the United Nations human development scale. It has the lowest life expectancy and the second lowest literacy level in Asia and the Pacific, one of the highest maternal and infant mortality rates in the world; hundreds of men, women and children are dying of AIDS each year and over 37 per cent of its population lives below the poverty line. Papua New Guinea citizens want to exercise self-determination rather than beg unscrupulous leaders for what is rightly theirs. Desperate for good health for their families, education and employment for their children and a more comfortable lifestyle they succumb, from time to time, to political and material compromise to obtain benefits. Such activity prolongs dependency upon aid agencies, and absorbs energy away from some very positive initiatives—neutralising both development and crime control efforts.

The control of crime in Papua New Guinea is not just a 'social' issue as politicians suggest. It is more a leadership issue which links with resource equity and availability, dictating state and community capacity. Neither state nor community controls that preserve human rights can work in isolation. State agencies and communities need to work together, their conjoint efforts sustained by a variety of state services and other resources. Universally, citizens want their leaders to lead and to create order. Papua New Guinea is no exception. They admire strength and consistency in leaders who have the courage of their convictions, high moral codes of behaviour, and offer visions that translate into practical benefits. To complement leadership, the public sector needs to be diligent in basic administrative practice, including the keeping of easily accessible filing systems, consistent reporting and recording of statistics, and regular monitoring and auditing of expenditure.

Crime control strategies will have more chance of working too when PNG citizens actively demand the prosecution of offenders against the public purse, when they actively demand that political integrity is regulated by law, and when they actively demand that the public sector implements procedures like the Office of Rural Development fraud control plan and the new Law and Order Policy which involves citizens in decision making. In such a transparent environment, resources will increase to communities, and citizens will have greater incentive to maintain order and to be enthusiastic practitioners of crime control strategies that respect shared values and beliefs—better linking with state-driven initiatives to preserve human rights.

References

Ahai, N., 2000. 'Focus', *Post-Courier*, 16 February:11.

Aleck, J., 1992. 'The village court system of Papua New Guinea', *Research in Melanesia,* 16, University of Papua New Guinea:101–28.

Ame, T., 2001. 'NCD among world's worst crime spots: sociologist', *The National*, 26–28 October:4.

Amet, A., 2000. 'Home News', *Post-Courier*, 1 March:3.

Arek, M., 2000. 'Capacity building gets priority', *Post-Courier,* 9 May:5.

August, D., 1998. Upcoming developments at Kerevat on unsolved and vigilant issues, minute to the Commissioner through AC-Support Services, PNGCS, 15 June.

AusAID, 1997. *One Clear Objective: poverty reduction through sustainable development*, report of the Committee of Review, April.

——, 1999. 'Asset maintenance: the impact of underfinancing of recurrent costs', *Quality Assurance Series,* 13, Canberra, May.

Australia Papua New Guinea Business Council, 1997. *Background on Law and Order Policy*, unsigned facsimile to the Registrar of the PNG National Courts, 21 May.

Baiom, M., 2000. 'Fighting for women', *Post-Courier*, 28 April:23.

References

Bande, J., 1997. Budget allocation request for PCCC youth activities, letter to the Madang Provincial Community Consultative Committee from Division of Administration Services, Office of Social Development, Madang Provincial Government, Papua New Guinea, 24 January.

Banks, C., 1993. *Women in Transition: social control in Papua New Guinea*, Australian Institute of Criminology, Canberra.

——, 2000. 'Contextualising sexual violence: rape and carnal knowledge in Papua New Guinea', in S. Dinnen and A. Ley, (eds), *Reflections on Violence in Melanesia,* Hawkins Press/Asia Pacific Press, Canberra:83–104.

Banks, G., 1996. 'Compensation for mining', in R. Howitt (ed.), *Resources, Nations and Indigenous Peoples,* Oxford University Press, Melbourne.

Barter, P., 1998. 'Public service wage rises', *Post-Courier*, 1 September:4.

Bayne, P., 1985. *Village Courts in Papua New Guinea,* paper delivered at Aboriginal Criminal Justice Workshop, The Australian National University, Canberra.

Becker, G. S., 1968. 'Crime and punishment', *Journal of Political Economy*, 76:169–217.

Biles, D., 1994. 'Effective countermeasures against crimes related to urbanisation and industrialisation—urban crime, juvenile delinquency and environmental crime', *Asia and Far East Institute for the Prevention of Crime and the Treatment of Offenders Report for 1993 and Resource Materials Series*, 45, United Nations Asia and Far East Institute for the Prevention of Crime and the Treatment of Offenders, Fuchu, Tokyo, December:152–69.

Black, D., 1976. *The Behaviour of Law,* Academic Press, New York.

Bonnell, S., 1999. 'Social change in the Porgera Valle' in C. Filer (ed.), *Dilemmas of Development: the social and economic impact of the Porgera gold mine 1989–94,* Asia Pacific Press, Asia Pacific School of Economic and Management (Pacific Policy Paper 34) and Resource Management in Asia-Pacific, Research School of Pacific and Asian Studies, The Australian National University and The National Research Institute, Boroko (Special Publication 24):128–59.

Borrey, A. 2000. 'Sexual violence in perspective: the case of Papua New Guinea', in S. Dinnen and A. Ley, (eds), *Reflections on Violence in Melanesia,* Hawkins Press/Asia Pacific Press, Canberra:105–18.

Borrey, A. and Sabadi, A., 1996. *Parole Research Project Report,* National Research Institute, Boroko, June.

Brooks, S., 1996. *Small Business Development in Papua New Guinea: lessons,* PNG Biodiversity Conservation and Resource Management Programme, Department of Environment and Conservation/United Nations Development Programme OPS–PNG/93/G31, Post Printing, Port Moresby.

Buchbinder, G., 1973. Maring micro-adaptation: a study of demographic, nutritional, genotypic and phenotypic variation in a highland New Guinea population, Columbia University (PhD thesis), New York.

Burns, R., 1995. *The Adult Learner at Work,* Business and Professional Publishing, Sydney.

Callaghan, M-L., 2001. '"Polies" plan to feather their nests gets PNG masses angry', *The Australian,* 14 February:8.

Campos, C.C., 1997. 'The fair and efficient administration of criminal justice: proper exercise of authority and procedural justice with emphasis on police discretion', *Asia and Far East Institute for the Prevention of Crime and the Treatment of Offenders Annual Report for 1995 and Resource Materials Series,* 49, United Nations Asia and Far East Institute for the Prevention of Crime and the Treatment of Offenders, Fuchu, Tokyo, February:56–68.

Chalmers, D., 1978. Full circle: a history of the courts of Papua New Guinea, University of Papua New Guinea (LIM thesis), Waigani:172–4.

Chan Kin-hung, A., 1996. 'The effective administration of criminal justice: public participation and prevention of corruption in Hong Kong', *Asia and Far East Institute for the Prevention of Crime and the Treatment of Offenders Annual Report and Resource Materials Series,* 48, United Nations Asia and Far East Institute for the Prevention of Crime and the Treatment of Offenders, Fuchu, Tokyo, March:104–20.

Chattoraj, B.N., 1996. 'Public participation in the treatment of offenders: an Indian perspective' *Asia and Far East Institute for the Prevention of Crime and the Treatment of Offenders Annual Report and Resource Materials Series,* 48, United Nations Asia and Far East Institute for the Prevention of Crime and the Treatment of Offenders, Fuchu, Tokyo, March:59–73.

Choi, N., 1998. 'Report queries 'unaccounted' funds', *The Independent,* 15 May:3.

——, 2000. 'Landowners losing out on log tax revenues', *The Independent,* 5 October:1.

Cleary, T., 1991. *The Art of War,* Shambhala Publications Inc., Boston.

Clifford, W., 1976. 'Urban crime in Papua New Guinea', in D. Biles (ed.), *Crime in Papua New Guinea,* Australian Institute of Criminology, Canberra:1–90.

——, 1984. 'The law and order project', *Institute of National Affairs Speech Series,* 29, Institute of National Affairs, Port Moresby, 1 August.

Clifford, W., Morauta, L. and Stuart, B., 1984a. 'Law and order in Papua New Guinea', *Volume I: report and recommendations,* Institute of National Affairs, Port Moresby.

——, 1984b. 'Law and order in Papua New Guinea', *Volume II: report and recommendations,* Institute of National Affairs, Port Moresby.

Clinard, M.B., 1976. 'The problem of crime and its control in developing countries', in D. Biles (ed.), *Crime in Papua New Guinea,* Australian Institute of Criminology, Canberra.

Connell, J., 1991. 'Compensation and conflict: the Bougainville copper mine, Papua New Guinea', in J. Connell, and R. Howitt (eds), *Mining and Indigenous Peoples in Australasia,* University of Sydney Press, Sydney.

Dau, J., 2001. 'Four PX staff raped in Pom', *The National,* 8 November:1.

Dauvergne, P., 1998. 'Weak states, strong states: a state-in-society perspective', in P. Dauvergne (ed.), *Weak and Strong States in Asia Pacific Societies,* Allen & Unwin Australia Pty Ltd, St Leonards.

Dennis, M., 1980. Melanesian migrants in towns ignore their cultural and social ties with their homes and have become committed town dwellers, essay comment on statement for the course of Melanesian Societies II, Faculty of Arts, University of Papua New Guinea, Boroko (unpublished).

——, 1981. 'Plantations', in D. Denoon and C. Snowden (eds), *A Time to Plant, A Time to Uproot,* University of Papua New Guinea Press, Waigani.

Department of Attorney-General, n.d. *Draft Corporate Plan 1998–2001,* Government of Papua New Guinea, Port Moresby.

Department of Home Affairs and Youth, 1987. *Women's Policy,* Government of Papua New Guinea, Port Moresby, 23 September:1–5.

Department of Justice, 1997. *District Court Criminal Records, 1997: judgements,* Government of Papua New Guinea, Port Moresby, 6 July.

Department of Provincial and Local Level Government Affairs, 1998. *Report on National Women's Policy and Status of Implementation,* Women's Division, Office of Family and Church, Government of Papua New Guinea, Port Moresby.

Diamond, J., 1991. *The Rise and Fall of the Third Chimpanzee,* Radius, London.

Dinnen, S., 1992. 'Crime, development and criminological research in Papua New Guinea', *National Research Institute Discussion Paper,* 66, Boroko.

——, 1993. 'Causes for concern: control talk in Papua New Guinea', *Taim Lain: A Journal of Contemporary Melanesian Studies,* Papua New Guinea, 1(1):13–37.

——, 1994a. *The Criminal Justice System of Papua New Guinea: a factual review,* National Research Institute, Papua New Guinea.

——, 1994b. 'Praise the Lord and pass the ammunition: criminal group surrender in Papua New Guinea', *National Research Institute Discussion Paper,* 81, Boroko, December:1–25.

——, 1998. 'In weakness and strength—state, societies and order in Papua New Guinea', in P. Dauvergne (ed.), *Weak and Strong States in Asia-Pacific Societies,* Allen & Unwin Australia Pty Ltd, St Leonards:38–59.

——, 1999. 'Criminal threats and the security of the State in Papua New Guinea', in B. Boeha (ed.), *Australia–Papua New Guinea: crime and the bilateral relationship,* National Research Institute Special Publication, 24, Boroko:36–46.

——, 2000. 'Violence and governance in Melanesia: an introduction', in S. Dinnen and A. Ley (eds), *Reflections on Violence in Melanesia,* Hawkins Press/Asia Pacific Press, Canberra:1–16.

Diro, E., 1998a. 'Poor leadership to blame for economic woes, says Diro'. *The National,* 2 September:11.

——, 1998b. 'An irrelevant parliament in a diminishing democracy', *The National,* 1 December:11.

Donigi, P., 1998. 'Donigi: politicians must pay for the mess we are in now', *Post-Courier,* 22 October:11.

Downs, I., 1980. *The Australian Trusteeship: Papua New Guinea 1945–75,* Department of Home Affairs, Australian Government Public Service, Canberra.

Dula Torres, E., 1996. 'The effective administration of criminal justice: public participation and prevention of corruption', *Asia and Far East Institute for the Prevention of Crime and the Treatment of Offenders Resource Materials Series,* 48, United Nations Asia and Far East Institute for the Prevention of Crime and the Treatment of Offenders, Fuchu, Tokyo, March:83–93.

Duncan, R., 2001. 'PNG economic survey: a scorecard for the Morauta administration', *Pacific Economic Bulletin,* 16(2):1–14

Duncan, R. and Lawson, T., 1997. 'Cost structures in Papua New Guinea', *Institute of National Affairs Discussion Paper,* 69, Port Moresby:1–116.

Duncan, R. and Xu, X., 1999. 'Should Papua New Guinea adopt a stronger exchange rate regime?', *Pacific Economic Bulletin,* 15(2):36–45.

Egan, K., 1992. 'An integrated national crime prevention policy and programme', *Foundation for Law, Order and Justice Policy Paper,* 1. Port Moresby.

Fallon, J. and Sugden, C., 1998. 'Papua New Guinea coping with shocks and achieving broad-based economic development', *Australian Agency for International Development, International Development Issues,* 52, May 1998, Economic Insights Pty Ltd, Canberra.

Filer, C., 1994. 'Socioeconomic impact assessment of the Tolukuma Gold Mine, Central Province', *Research in Melanesia,* Boroko.

Firth, S., 1986. *New Guinea Under the Germans,* Web Books, Hong Kong.

Fowler, H.W. and Fowler, F.G., (eds), 1976. *The Concise Oxford Dictionary of Current English: based on the Oxford English Dictionary and its supplements,* sixth edition J. B. Sykes (ed.), Oxford at the Clarendon Press:252.

Gammage, B., 1996. 'Police and power during contact in the New Guinea Highlands', in H. Levine and A. Ploeg (eds.), *Work in Progress: essays in New Guinea Highlands ethnography in honour of Paula Brown Glick,* Peter Lang, Frankfurt.

Garnaut, R., 1979. *The Urban Household Survey: town profiles,* Institute of Applied Social and Economic Research (IASER), Monograph 12, Boroko, Papua New Guinea:2–6.

Gerawa, M., 1998. 'Report says PNG is undeveloped', *Post-Courier,* 25 September:5.

——, 2000. 'Terror at Gerehu', *Post-Courier,* 5 April:1.

Gibson, J. and Rozelle, S., 1998. *Results of the Household Survey Component of the 1996 Povrty Assessment for Papua New Guinea,* J. Gibson, Poverty and Human Resources Division, East Asia and the Pacific Department, The World Bank, Washington, DC.

Goddard, M., 1992a. 'Of handcuffs and foodbaskets: theory and practice in Papua New Guinea's village courts', *Research in Melanesia,* 16:79–94.

——, 1992b. 'Bigman thief: the social origin of gangs in Port Moresby', *Canberra Anthropology,* 15(1):20–34.

——, 1995. 'The rascal road: crime, prestige, and development in Papua New Guinea', *The Contemporary Pacific,* 7(1):55–80.

——, 1996. 'The snake bone case: law, custom, and justice in a Papua New Guinea village court', *Oceania,* 67(1):50–63.

——, 1998. 'Off the record: village court praxis and the politics of settlement life in Port Moresby, Papua New Guinea', *Canberra Anthropology,* 21(1):41–62.

Gomez, B., 2001. 'Economy in dire straits', *The National,* 26 October:4.

Gordon, R.J. and Meggitt, M.J., 1985. *Law and Order in the New Guinea Highlands: encounters with Enga,* University Press of New England, Hanover.

Government of Papua New Guinea, 1975. *Constitution of the Independent State of Papua New Guinea 1975,* Government of Papua New Guinea, Port Moresby, Section 55.

——, 1994–97. *Short Interim Report on the Restructured System of Provincial and Local-Level Governments*, Constitutional Review Commission Reports, Volume 1, Port Moresby, 30 June.

——, 1995. *Correctional Service Act 1995 No. 6 of 1995*, Port Moresby, (certified on 15 May 1995).

——, 1996a. *Organic Law on Provincial and Local Level Governments 1996,* Government of Papua New Guinea, Port Moresby, May.

——, 1996b. *Short Interim Report on the Re-structured System of Provincial and Local-Level Governments,* Constitutional Review Commission Reports 1994–97, Volume 1, Port Moresby, 30 June.

——, 1997. *Targeted Community Development Program Overview and Project Application,* Government of Papua New Guinea, Port Moresby, August:2–8.

——, 1999. *Memorandum of Understanding between Provincial Governments and Papua New Guinea Correctional Service,* Proforma Memorandum of Understanding, Government of Papua New Guinea, Port Moresby.

——, 1989. *Village Court Act of Papua New Guinea 1989,* Government of Papua New Guinea, Section 52, 61–2.

Grabosky, P.N., 1996. *Public Participation and Co-operation in Crime Prevention Activities*, Asia and Far East Institute for the Prevention of Crime and the Treatment of Offenders Resource Materials Series, 48, United Nations Asia and Far East Institute for the Prevention of Crime and the Treatment of Offenders, Fuchu, Tokyo, March:33–47.

Griffin, J., Nelson, H. and Firth, S., 1999. *Papua New Guinea: a political history*, Heinemann educational Australia, Melbourne.

Gustafsson, B., 1999. *Traditions and Modernities in Gender Roles: transformations in kinship and marriage among the M'buke from Manus Province,* National Research Institute Monograph 35, The National Research Institute, Boroko.

Haiveta, C., 1997. 'A vision for Papua New Guinea', in I. Temu (ed.), *Papua New Guinea: a 20/20 vision,* National Centre for Development Studies, Research School of Pacific and Asian Studies, The Australian National University, Canberra, (Pacific Policy Paper 20) and National Research Institute, Boroko (NRI Special Publication 22).

Harden, R., 1999. 1999 Economic Report Executive Summary, presented at the PNG Economic Update Seminar, Islander Hotel, Port Moresby, 16 November.

Harris, B.M., 1998. *The Rise of Rascalism*, National Research Institute Discussion Paper 54, The National Research Institute, Boroko.

Hiambohn, W., 1998a. 'Economic adviser's K7m deal', *Post-Courier*, 11–13 September:1.

——, 1998b. 'Report on corruption cites major problems', *Post-Courier*, 24 September:3.

——, 1999a. 'PM: NPF abused', *Post-Courier*, 29 October:1.

——, 1999b. 'NARI chief gets sack', *Post-Courier*, 8 January:2.

——, 1999c. 'Government must take full responsibility', *Post-Courier*, 16 February:2.

——, 2000a. 'Debate on who gets more from Australia aid to PNG', *Post-Courier*, 13 March:2.

——, 2000b. 'Most MPs have guns says PM', *Post-Courier*, 26 April:1.

——, 2000c. 'Save PNG: MPs', *Post-Courier*, 9 May:1.

——, 2000d. 'Marijuana vice deeply rooted', *Post-Courier*, 11 May:1.

——, 2000e. 'State bodies 'technically' bankrupt', *Post-Courier*, 13 October:5.

Hukula, F., 1999. *Women and Security in Port Moresby*, National Research Institute Discussion Paper No. 92, The National Research Institute, Boroko, April.

Hunt, C., 1998. *Pacific Development Sustained: policy for Pacific environments*, National Centre for Development Studies Pacific Policy Paper 32, Asia Pacific Press, The Australian National University, Canberra.

——, 1999a. 'Public spending from taxation', *Post-Courier*, 12 November:11.

——, 1999b. 'Implementing a public investment policy', *Post-Courier*, 29 November:11.

——, 1999c. 'Behind the budget focus', *Post-Courier*, 8 December:11.

——, 1999d. 'Making slush funds work', *Post-Courier*, 9 December:11.

——, 2000. 'The NFP—its past, present and future', *Post-Courier*, 4 May:11.

——, 2001. 'Roads to ruin', *Post-Courier*, 31 October:11.

Hunt, C., Mawuli, A., Gumoi, M., Yala, C. and Sanida, O., 1999. 'Public investment policy in Papua New Guinea', *Pacific Economic Bulletin*, 14(2):24–36.

Hunt, C. and Wangi, J., 1997. Results of a pilot survey of traditional coastal villages of the National Capital District, Health Hazards Study Report 1 (unpublished).

Inguba, S., 1999. 'Bilateral co-operation in cross-border crime', in B. Boeha (ed.), *Australia–Papua New Guinea: crime and the bilateral relationship,* The National Research Institute Special Publication 24, Boroko:48–53.

Institute of National Affairs, 1999a. *Speech Series,* 1, Aviat Club, Port Moresby, 9 February.

Institute of National Affairs, 1999b. *Factors Contributing to the Lack of Investment in Papua New Guinea: a private sector survey*, Institute of National Affairs Discussion Paper 74, Port Moresby.

Jalal, P., 1999. Commonwealth Mission, 22–26 February, 1999, letter to Commissioner, PNG Correctional Service from Office of Director, Office of Family and Church Affairs, Department of Provincial and Local Government Affairs, Port Moresby.

Japan International Cooperation Agency (JICA), 1997. 'Carp for the villagers', *Passion in the Pacific*, JICA Newsletter, 7(2):4–5.

Jessep, O., 1991. 'Customary family law, women's rights, and village courts in Papua New Guinea', *Melanesian Law Journal,* 19:65–77.

Jimu, A., 1989. 'Criminal justice system in Papua New Guinea', *Asia and Far East Institute for the Prevention of Crime and the Treatment of Offenders Resource Materials Series* 36, United Nations Asia and Far East Institute for the Prevention of Crime and the Treatment of Offenders, Fuchu, Tokyo, December:247–51.

Jinks, B., Biskup, P. and Nelson, H., 1973. *Readings in New Guinea History,* Angus and Robertson, Brisbane.

Joku, F., 1999a. 'Public funds used to meet poll costs', *The National,* 18 February:2.

——, 1999b. 'Pundari out', *The National,* 9–10 December:1.

Kalasim, H. R., 1997. Budget allocation request for PCCC youth activities, letter from the Madang Police Community Consultative Committee to Mr. Joe Bandi of the Madang Youth Services, Madang Provincial Government, Madang, 16 January.

Kapigeno, J., 1999. 'Poverty is high, says World Bank', *Post-Courier,* 25 October:2.

Kaputin, Sir J., 1999. 'Home news', *Post-Courier,* 14 June:3.

——, 2000. 'Governance in the 21st Century', *Post-Courier,* 1 May:11.

Kare, K., 2000, 'PNG is old enough to deliver services', *Post-Courier,* 20 April:10.

Karella, K. and Whittaker, M., 1998. *Report on the Status of Nine Correctional Institutions with Recommendations for Action,* PNG Correctional Service, Government of Papua New Guinea, Port Moresby, 10 February.

Kaye, M., 1992. 'Communication competence', in A. Gonczi (ed.), *Developing a Competent Workforce,* National Centre for Vocational education Research, Adelaide:80–104.

Kenneth, G., 2000. 'Population boom', *Post-Courier,* 22–24 September:1.

King, T., 1997. 'Structural reform versus stabilisation', in I. Temu (ed.), *Papua New Guinea: a 20/20 vision,* National Centre for Development Studies, Research School of Pacific and Asian Studies, The Australian National University, Canberra, (Pacific Policy Paper 20) and National Research Institute, Boroko (NRI Special Publication No. 22).

Kirschmann, G.J. and Kirschmann, J.D., 1996. *Nutrition Almanac,* Fourth edition, McGraw-Hill, New York.

Kituai, A., 1988. 'Innovation and intrusion: villages and policemen in Papua New Guinea', *Journal of Pacific History,* 23(2):156–66.

——, 1998. *My Gun, My Brother: the world of the Papua New Guinea colonial police 1920–60,* University of Hawaii Press Honolulu.

Koimanrea, F., 1998. Speech by the Honourable Francis Koimanrea, MP, Governor of East New Britain Province on the occasion of the official opening of Toguata Police Barracks, The Regional/Provincial Police Headquarters and Kokopo Police Station, Baliora Township, Kokopo, East New Britain, 14 May.

Kone, E., 2000. 'NPF debt now K34m: Mitchell', *The National,* 6 October:2.

——, 2001. 'K35m gift', *Post-Courier,* 31 October:1.

Kuble, E. and Godfrid, H., 1999. 'North Simbu Rural Development Project', *The National,* 19 August.

Kumar, A., 1997. 'Crime prevention: the administration of criminal justice II',. *Asia and Far East Institute for the Prevention of Crime and the Treatment of Offenders Resource Materials Series* 49, United Nations Asia and Far East Institute for the Prevention of Crime and the Treatment of Offenders, Fuchu, Tokyo, February:143–53.

Kwara, T., 1999. 'New party is formed', *The National,* 10 December:2.

Larmour, P., 1998. 'Migdal in Melanesia', in P. Dauvergne (ed.), *Weak and Strong States in Asia Pacific Societies,* Allen & Unwin in association with Department of International Relations, Research School of Pacific and Asian Studies, The Australian National University, Canberra:77–92.

Law Reform Commission of Papua New Guinea, 1987. *Interim Report on Domestic Violence,* Law Reform Commission of Papua New Guinea, Boroko.

Legal Institutions Strengthening Project, 1997a. *Draft Project Design Document,* Volume 1 Annexures, Australian Agency for International Development (AusAID), November.

——, 1997b. *Draft Project Design Document,* Volume 2 Annexures, Australian Agency for International Development (AusAID), February.

Lepani, B., 1993. 'Troubled but robust land', in M.J. Bourke, S. Holzknecht, K. Kituai and L. Roach (eds), *Our Time But Not Our Place,* Melbourne University Press, Melbourne:69–81.

Levantis, T., 1997. 'Urban unemployment in Papua New Guinea: it's criminal', *Pacific Economic Bulletin,* 12(2):73–84.

——, 2000. 'Crime catastrophe—reviewing Papua New Guinea's most serious social and economic problem', *Pacific Economic Bulletin* 15(2):130–42.

Levantis, T. and Chand, S., 1997. Crime and optimal expenditure on deterrence: the case of Papua New Guinea, presented at a conference on Crime in Papua New Guinea, National Centre for Development Studies, The Australian National University, Canberra, June.

Levantis, T. and Fane, G., 1997. *Labour Market Regulation and Deregulation in Papua New Guinea,* Economics Division, Research School of Pacific and Asian Studies, The Australian National University, Canberra.

Magun, W., 1998. 'PNG lacks sufficient fiscal policy', *Business News,* 29 May:17.

Manning, M., 1999a. 'We differ from other developing nations', *Post-Courier,* 8 January:11.

——, 1999b. 'Where our economy really stands', *Post-Courier,* 5 February:11.

——, 2000a. 'Why we need the informal sector', *Post-Courier,* 28 April:11.

——, 2000b. 'Why are people poor?', *Post-Courier,* 12 May:11.

Mato Business and Development Consultancy, 1999. *A Proposal to Conduct Entrepreneurial Skills Training for Inmates in Papua New Guinea Goals,* Mato Business and Development Consultancy, Lae.

Mawuli, A. and Dzuali, R.R., 1993. *Economic Participation of Residents in Selected Communities in Port Moresby,* Development Support Services (DSS) of the United Nations Development Programme and presented at the launching of the United Nations Development Programme 1993 Human Development Report at Port Moresby, 1 July.

May, R., 1998. 'State, society and governance: reflections on a Philippines–Papua New Guinea comparison', in P. Dauvergne (ed.), *Weak and Strong States in Asia-Pacific Societies,* Allen & Unwin in association with Department of International Relations, Research School of Pacific and Asian Studies, The Australian National University, Canberra:60–76.

Minimum Wages Board (MWB), 1974, *Determination No. 3,* Minimum Wages Board, Waigani.

——, 1992. *Determination 1992,* Minimum Wages Board, Waigani.

Mohan, C., 1996. 'Countermeasures to the abuse of power and corruption: some lessons from Singapore', *Asia and Far East Institute for the Prevention of Crime and the Treatment of Offenders Resource Materials Resource Materials* 48, United Nations Asia and Far East Institute for the Prevention of Crime and the Treatment of Offenders, Fuchu, Tokyo, March:74 82.

Narayan, D., 1995. *The Contribution of People's Participation: evidence from 121 rural water supply projects,* Environmental Sustainable Development Occasional Paper 1, The World Bank, Washington, DC.

National Court, 1997. *Case of Murder,* District Court files, judgement handed down on 6 July.

National Statistical Office, 1995. *People Count,* summary of the 1990 Population and Housing Census in Papua New Guinea, United Nations Population Fund, Port Moresby, March.

——, 2001. *Preliminary Figures,* Papua New Guinea 2000 Census, National Statistical Office, Port Moresby, May.

Nicholas, I., 2000. 'PM fires 3 ministers', *The National,* 10–12 March:1.

Nonggorr, J., 1998a. 'Defining the law', *The National,* 8 July:15.

——, 1998b. 'Significance of our constitution', *The National,* 12 August:17.

——, 1998c. 'Our rights under constitution', *The National,* 26 August:15.

——, 1998d. 'The major offices under constitution', *The National,* 2 September:15.

——, 1998e. 'The Sandline probe findings', *The National,* 21 October:17.

——, 1998f. 'Problem areas of law in Papua New Guinea', *The National,* 25 November:17.

——, 1998g. 'Sandline affair and reforms', *The National,* 2 December:17.

——, 1998h. 'Spotlight on law', *The National,* 8 December:15.

——, 1999. 'Inquiries galore—but no action', *The National,* 17 November:15.

O'Connell, C., and Zarriga, R.I., 1991. 'Papua New Guinea's national youth movement', in S. Sewell and A. Kelly (eds), *Social Problems in the Asia Pacific Region,* Boolarong Publishers, Brisbane:211–41.

Office of International Development Assistance, 1993. *Report on Foreign Aid,* Department of Finance and Planning, Waigani, September.

Office of National Planning, 1999a. *Brief on Papua New Guinea's Development Co-operation Program with its Bilateral Aid Donors,* Bilateral Branch of the Foreign Aid Management Division, Government of Papua New Guinea, Port Moresby.

——, 1999b. *Papua New Guinea Human Development Report 1998,* Government of Papua New Guinea and United Nations Development Programme, Port Moresby, September.

Office of National Planning and Transparency International Inc, 2000. Privatisation and the Integrity Pact Forum, Granville Hotel, Port Moresby, 28 February.

Office of the Prime Minister, 2001a. *NEC Withdraws Enga Powers,* available online at http://www.pm.gov.pmsoffice.

——, 2001b. *Defence Reform Proposals Approved,* available online at http://www.pm.gov.pmsoffice.

——, 2001c. *Philemon Pleased with Successful Outcome of Ministerial Forum,* available online at http://www.pm.gov.pmsoffice.

Office of Rural Development, 2000a. *Draft Fraud Control Plan,* Government of Papua New Guinea, Port Moresby, March:3–7.

——, 2000b. *Working Draft of the District Development Program Social and Rural Development Grant Guidelines for the fiscal year 2000,* Government of Papua New Guinea, Port Moresby, March:5–10.

Oram, N.D., 1976. *Colonial Town to Melanesian City,* The Australian National University Press, Canberra.

Ove, D., 1999. *Proposal for Recruiting Ex-Prisoners or Convicts for Rehabilitation and Training Purposes,* Port Moresby Youth Training Centre, Port Moresby.

Palme, W., 1998. 'Poverty level up in villages', *Post-Courier,* 24 September:2.

Pamba, K., 1999. 'Righting the budget wrongs', *The National,* 4 November:15.

Papua New Guinea Correctional Service (PNGCS), 1997. *Detainee Admissions,* Operations Division, Port Moresby.

——, 1998a. *Briefing Paper to Minister for Correctional Service from Commissioner for Correctional Service on Transfer of Parole Function to the Department of Correctional Service,* Port Moresby, 5 May.

——, 1998b. Transfer of probation, parole, community work and juvenile functions to Department of Correctional Service, (Commissioner's verbal brief), Port Moresby, 17 August.

——, 1998c. *Organizational Climate Survey Summary of Responses,* Operations Branch, Papua New Guinea Correctional Service, Port Moresby, August.

——, 1998d. *Detainee Admissions,* Operations Division, Port Moresby.

——, 1999. *Detainee Admissions,* Operations Division, Port Moresby.

——, 2001. *Corporate Plan 1999-2001,* Port Moresby.

Parkop, P. and Roywoiwabal, M., 1998. 'Who caused the Sandline crisis and threatened democracy!', *The National,* 11 November:17.

Paska, J., 1999. 'Privatisation and the pitfalls of classic liberalism: a case for state's role in economy', *The National,* 12 November:19.

Philemon, O., 2000. 'Gun held at Labi', *Post-Courier,* 7–9 January:1.

Philip, L., 1999. 'What is democracy?', *Post-Courier,* 19 February:10.

Pitts, M., 1999a. *Welfare and Rehabilitation Quarterly Report: March, April May 1999,* Correctional Service Development Project, Port Moresby, 21 May.

——, 1999b. *Annual Report Welfare and Rehabilitation: July 1998–June 1999,* Correctional Service Development Project, Port Moresby, 2 July.

——, 1999c. *Pilot Prison Industry Progress & Project Impact: 1997 to 1999,* Correctional Service Development Project, Port Moresby.

——, 1999d. *Progress in Prison Industry Pilot Projects: evaluation report,* PNG Correctional Service, Port Moresby, August.

——, 1999e. *Prisoner Development & Rehabilitation Programs in Core Prisons: evaluation report,* PNG Correctional Service, Port Moresby, September.

——, 1999f. *Schemes to Utilise Prison Labour for Community Projects: evaluation report,* PNG Correctional Service, Port Moresby, September.

——, 1999g. *Progress in Establishing Links with Non-Government Organizations: evaluation report,* PNG Correctional Service, Port Moresby, September.

Podolefsky, A. M., 1978. Pattern, process and decision making in New Guinea Highlands dispute handling, unpublished Doctoral dissertation, State University, Stony Brook, New York.

Poiya, J., 2000. 'Nurses raped', *Post-Courier,* 10 October:1.

Print, 1993. *Curriculum Development and Design,* Allen & Unwin, Sydney.

Raka, L.L., 1997. *Combined Annual Brief for 1996 and 1997,* Policy and Planning Division, National Court Registry, Papua New Guinea.

Rannells, J., 1995. *Papua New Guinea: a fact book on modern Papua New Guinea,* second edition, Oxford University Press, Melbourne.

Reuben, D. KII, 1999. 'School burnt as tribal war rages', *The National,* 11 December:2.

Ricketts, K., 2000. 'PNG's leader tossed into national "bearpit"', *Post-Courier,* 13–15 October:2.

Roy, A., 1999. *The Cost of Living,* Flamingo, London.

Royal Papua New Guinea Constabulary (RPNGC), 1998. *Development Project, Phase II, Quarterly Report for period January 1 to March 31,* Quarter 21, RPNGC, Port Moresby.

——, 2001a. *Royal Papua New Guinea Constabulary Strategic Plan 1997–2001,* RPNGC, Port Moresby.

——, 2001b. *Simbu Province 1997–2001 Strategic Plan,* RPNGC, Port Moresby.

——, 2001c. *Community Policing Directorate 1999–2001,* strategic plan: annexure 'DA', RPNGC, Port Moresby.

——, 2001d. *Corporate Plan 1997–2001,* RPNGC, Port Moresby, 26 July.

Sah, R. K., 1991. 'Social osmosis and patterns of crime', *Journal of Political Economy,* 99(6):1272–95.

Salafsky, N., 1997. *Eleven Steps for Setting up Community-Based Timber Harvesting Enterprises: an overview of the IRECDP experience in the islands region, Papua New Guinea,* European Union–Islands Region Environment and Community Development Programme, Biodiversity Conservation Network (BCN), Washington, DC.

Sekhran, N. and McCallum, R., 1996. Lessons learned through ICAD experimentation in Papua New Guinea: the Lak experience, paper to the UNDP Heads of Forestry Meeting, Port Vila, Vanuatu (unpublished).

Sela, R., 1999a. 'Govt blamed for crime rise', *Post-Courier,* 19 February:2.

——, 1999b. 'Ex-PM faces fraud charge', *Post-Courier,* 22 November:1.

——, 2000a. 'Crime keeping investors out', *Post-Courier,* 10 March:1.

——, 2000b. 'Karani banks death chair', *Post-Courier,* 25 April:1.

——, 2000c. 'Motor vehicle trust bankrupt', *Post-Courier,* 2 October:1.

Senge, F., 2000. 'Barakau paradise', *The National,* 10–12 March:3.

Sere, M. A., 1996. 'The effective administration of criminal justice: public articipation, the prevention of corruption and the Ombudsman Commission of Papua New Guinea connection', *Asia and Far East Institute for the Prevention of Crime and the Treatment of Offenders Resource Materials Series* 48, United Nations Asia and Far East Institute for the Prevention of Crime and the Treatment of Offenders, Fuchu, Tokyo, March:135–45.

Siaguru, Sir A., 1999. 'War of "haves" and "have nots"', *Post-Courier,* 4 June:11.

——, 2000a. 'The people's PM', *Post-Courier,* 28 January:11.

——, 2000b. 'Focus', *Post-Courier,* 28 January:11.

——, 2000c. 'Focus', *Post-Courier,* 2 February:10.

——, 2000d. 'Sad Truth', *Post-Courier,* 20 April:11.

Sikani, R., 1996. Dealing with deviance in contemporary Papua New Guinea societies: the choice of sanctions in village and local court proceedings, Master of Arts Thesis, University of Melbourne, Australia.

——, 1999. 'Criminal threat in Papua New Guinea', in B. Boeha (ed.), *Australia-Papua New Guinea: crime and the bilateral relationship,* National Research Institute Special Publication 24, Boroko:12–35.

——, 2000. 'Focus', *Post-Courier,* 30 March:11.

Simons, H., 1997. *One Clear Objective: poverty reduction through sustainable development,* Report of the Committee of Review, The Australian Overseas Aid Program, AusAID, Canberra, April.

Soetjipto, H.A.A., 1990. 'Incorporation of fair and effective crime prevention policies and strategies into overall national development plans', *Asia and Far East Institute for the Prevention of Crime and the Treatment of Offenders Report for 1989 and Resource Materials Series* 37, United Nations Asia and Far East Institute for the Prevention of Crime and the Treatment of Offenders, Fuchu, Tokyo, April:102–13.

Strathern, M., 1972. 'Official and unofficial courts: legal assumptions and expectations in a Highlands Community', *New Guinea Research Bulletin* 47, Port Moresby.

——, 1976. 'Crime and corrections: the place of prisons in Papua New Guinea', *Melanesian Law Journal,* 4(1):67–93.

——, 1977. 'The disconcerting tie: attitudes of Hagen migrants towards home', in R.J. May (ed.), *Change and Movement,* Australian National University Press, Canberra.

Taimbari, C., 1998. 'PM Skate: I had no confidence in General Nuia', *Post-Courier,* 15 October:2.

——, 2000a. 'Selfish motives lead to crises at the top', *Post-Courier,* 9 May:4.

——, 2000b. 'Kumuls woes', *Post-Courier,* 6–8 October:1.

——, 2001. 'Media campaign needed for 'vote' in 2007 national election', *The National,* 26–28 October:5

Temane, T., 1998. 'Doubt over Integrity Bill', *Post-Courier,* 22 October:3.

Tisdell, C.A., 1996. *Local Communities, Conservation and Sustainability: institutional change, altered governance and Kant's social philosophy,* Department of Economics Discussion Paper 205, The University of Queensland, Brisbane, September.

Togarewa, N., 1998. 'Public sector must be accountable', *The National,* 14 December:4.

Togarewa, N. and Isaac, N., 1998. 'Reckless and deceitful budget, says Philemon', *The National,* 25 November:2.

Torres, E.D., 1996. 'The effective administration of criminal justice: public participation and the prevention of corruption', *Asia and Far East Institute for the Prevention of Crime and the Treatment of Offenders Resource Materials Series* 48, United Nations Asia and Far East Institute for the Prevention of Crime and the Treatment of Offenders, Fuchu, Tokyo, March:83–93.

Turner, M., 1990. *Papua New Guinea: the challenge of independence,* Penguin Books, Melbourne.

Tuta, R., 1997. Application for volunteers house development with simple village base planning and initiations for recommendation to big aid donors like AusAID, JICA, EEC, etc, Baniamta Clan, Kambaramba Village, Angoram, East Sepik Province, 27 March.

United Nations Asia and Far East Institute for the Prevention of Crime and the Treatment of Offenders (UNAFEI), 1995. 'Report of the course: fauds against enterprises and consumers', *UNAFEI Report for 1994 and Resource Materials Series* 47, United Nations Asia and Far East Institute for the Prevention of Crime and the Treatment of Offenders, Fuchu, Tokyo, December:221–37.

United Nations Development Programme, 1994. *Pacific Human Development Report,* United Nations Development Programme, Suva:74–5, Tables A1–A3.

——, 1999. *Papua New Guinea Human Development Report 1998,* Office of National Planning, Government of Papua New Guinea, September.

UNICEF, 1996. *Children, Women and Families in Papua New Guinea: a situation analysis,* Government of Papua New Guinea and United Nations International Children's Fund, Port Moresby.

United States Department of State, 1999. *Papua New Guinea Country Report on Human Rights Practices for 1998,* released by the Bureau of Democracy, Human Rights and Labor, Washington, DC, 26 February.

Vai'i, D., 1998. 'Born to suffer tells of the unfortunate in PNG', *Post-Courier,* 24 November:23.

Valentine, C., 1963. An introduction to the history of changing ways of life on the Island of New Britain, PhD Thesis, University of Pennsylvania, Boston:107–8.

Van Helden, F., 1998. *Between Cash and Conviction: the social context of the Bismarck–Ramu Integrated Conservation and Development Project,* United Nations Development Programme (Global Environment Facility UNOPS–PNG/93/G31), The National Research Institute, Boroko (NRI Monograph 33).

Waiko, J. D., 1993. *A Short History of Papua New Guinea,* Oxford University Press, Melbourne.

Wale, P., 2000. 'Politicians up to no good again', *The National,* 5 October:13.

Waram, R., 2001a. 'Domestic funding mooted', *Post-Courier,* 31 October:3.

——, 2001b. 'All doom and gloom for us', *Post-Courier,* 1 November:1.

Wari, K., 1998. Presentation to Papua New Guinea Correctional Service Commanders' Conference, Bluff Inn, Sogeri, Papua New Guinea, 14 October.

Wood, J.W., 1980. Mechanisms of demographic equilibrium in a small human population: the Gainj of Papua New Guinea, University of Michigan (PhD Thesis), Ann Arbor.

Wolfers, E.P., 1975. *Race Relations and Colonial Rule in Papua New Guinea,* Australia and New Zealand Book Company, Sydney.

World Bank, 1993. *Staff Appraisal Report Papua New Guinea: population and family planning project,* Report No. 11264–PNG.

——, 1999. *Papua New Guinea: improving governance and performance. Poverty Reduction and Economic Management Sector Unit East Asia and Pacific Region,* Report No. 19388–PNG.

Yadi, A., 2001. 'Rape sparks revenge "raid"', *Post-Courier,* 6 November:3.

Zvekic, U. and Alvazzi, A., 1995. *Criminal Victimisation in the Developing World,* Interregional Crime and Justice Research Institute, New York.

Zvekic, U. and Weatherburn, D.J., 1993. *Strategy and Mechanisms for Development and Co-ordination of Crime and Criminal Justice Statistics in Papua New Guinea,* United Nations Interregional Crime and Justice Research Institute, Rome, October.

——, 1995. *Crime and Criminal Justice Information in Papua New Guinea,* Interregional Crime and Justice Research Institute, New York.